BARBECUE LOVER'S
MEMPHIS AND
TENNESSEE STYLES

BARBECUE LOVER'S
MEMPHIS AND
TENNESSEE STYLES

Restaurants, Markets, Recipes & Traditions

Stephanie Stewart-Howard

Globe
Pequot

GUILFORD, CONNECTICUT

To my husband, Seth Howard, without whom I'd never be able to do this, and to my dad, Joe Stewart, without whom I'd know nothing about barbecue.

Globe Pequot

An imprint of Rowman & Littlefield

Distributed by NATIONAL BOOK NETWORK

Copyright © 2015 by Rowman & Littlefield

All photography by the author unless otherwise noted.

Maps: Alena Joy Pearce © Rowman & Littlefield

British Library Cataloguing in Publication Information Available

Library of Congress Cataloging-in-Publication Data
Stewart-Howard, Stephanie.
  Barbecue lover's Memphis and Tennessee styles : restaurants, markets, recipes & traditions / Stephanie Stewart-Howard.
      pages cm
  Includes index.
  ISBN 978-1-4930-0636-6 (pbk.) — ISBN 978-1-4930-1902-1 (e-book)
  1. Barbecuing—Tennessee—Memphis. 2. Restaurants—Tennessee—Memphis.
  3. Barbecuing—Tennessee. 4. Restaurants—Tennessee. I. Title.
  TX840.B3S75 2015
  641.7'60976819—dc23

2015015986

∞™ The paper used in this publication meets the minimum requirements of American National Standard for Information Sciences—Permanence of Paper for Printed Library Materials, ANSI/NISO Z39.48-1992.

All the information in this guidebook is subject to change. We recommend that you call ahead to obtain current information before traveling.

CONTENTS

ABOUT THE AUTHOR

Stephanie Stewart-Howard is a journalist and author whose résumé also includes work as an artist, actor, costume designer, and researcher. After spending several years as managing editor and primary writer at *Nashville Lifestyles* magazine, she decided to leap into the book and freelance world. She is the author of *Nashville Chef's Table*. She currently contributes regularly to *12th and Broad*, *Nashville Arts Magazine*, *Renaissance* magazine, Livability.com, *Where Nashville*, and a host of other local and national publications. She lives in Franklin, Tennessee, with her husband and two cats.

ACKNOWLEDGMENTS

This book would never have happened without the help and advice of some amazing people.

Pat and Martha Martin, you guys are the best for so many reasons. In a lot of ways, you started this book for me years before I came to write it, and your food sustained me through the composition of it. I could never have done this without you.

Carey Bringle, thanks for recipes, food when I needed it, and fantastic interviews. You've inspired me in so many ways with your cool attitude and your truly excellent ribs.

Chris Chamberlain, Thomas Williams, Nick Pihakis, Jim Myers, John T. Edge: guys, I think I have to buy you all a beer. Thank you so much for helping me out in the early stages of this book.

Jason Little, Daisy King, Ray DuBose, and Carl T. Atkins, for inspired recipes.

Carson Reed, Vincent Farone, Sean Reisz, and Bill Howell, thanks for being my daily inspirations in the world of home barbecue. I've learned a whole lot from each of you over the years.

To my mom, Yvonne Stewart, for encouragement and the occasional glass of Riesling, judiciously applied.

To the wondrous Ms. Shawn Reed, thanks for hitting the trails in the park with me and letting me clear my head.

And to all the other girls who keep me sane and help me out: my sister Laura Holder, my aunt, Jackie Howell, and my friends Jennifer Matthews, Lara Olstad, Hilary Yodis, Amy Ripton, Kelley Davidson, Kathy Aslinger, Dena Nance, Michaela Burnham, Amy-Renee King, TJ Vestal, Jenny Barnhill, Kendra Greathouse, Diana Ellis, Bridget Dohaney, and all the rest of you.

FRESH
BEST IN TOWN!

INTRODUCTION

Driving down the road in Tennessee, no matter where you go, there's a barbecue joint in the immediate vicinity. Some are big, spacious, and pretty; others are small, set in shacks or old gas stations. The appearance gives little away about the quality of the barbecue. Sometimes, the shack with the smoker produces the best food you've ever tasted. But one thing is certain: We're serious about our barbecue around here, big joint or small.

As I write this, the long history of the really good, filling, moderately priced pulled pork sandwich from so many of these joints is being called into question by record pork prices, caused in part by issues of disease and drought across the pig-raising parts of the nation. But whatever comes of that, rest assured that the barbecue gods of Tennessee are going to do their best to keep producing something tender, juicy, and rich on your palate that doesn't break the bank.

It says a great deal that we must now discuss the reality of our changing foodways and the shifts being caused by the market and a new understanding

of food production—but those things are impacting the way we consume and select foods. As a national conversation arises about the origins of our food and the way we source it, it affects barbecue—from the big chains to the tiny shacks with smokers outside—in ways we might not have anticipated a decade or more ago.

Things like whole hog, once a given, have started fading from the culture because of issues of supply and the reality that in this day and age, it's just more cost effective to smoke butts and shoulders. Of perhaps greater concern is the decline of the family farm and the closing of US Department of Agriculture (USDA) plants, making it harder and more expensive for small restaurants to source those whole hogs. But more on that later.

Of course, globalization on a big scale impacts the local barbecue culture too—the proliferation of information at your fingertips via the Internet, the rise of big barbecue competitions, and the shrinking size of the world mean that regional types of barbecue start to blend together in ways they hadn't before, and the definitions that once seemed so clear have softer edges. It may not be surprising that you can find "Tennessee-" or "Memphis"-style barbecue in New York, but for some, it jars that you can find it in Dallas or Kansas City—or those types of barbecue here in Nashville, Knoxville, and Memphis.

But then, what is Tennessee barbecue at the root? John T. Edge of the Southern Foodways Alliance is pretty insistent to me that there's no single definition of the barbecue from the Tennessee region because we have an interesting mix of urban and rural traditions that have grown up and intermingled with and been influenced by the rise of the huge barbecue competitions and, even more, by changing demographics that moved people around and closed those plants that produced whole hog in West Tennessee. He has his own detailed and profound commentary on the subject, which I urge you to read.

When it comes to Memphis and the notion of "Memphis barbecue," Jim Holt, chief executive officer (CEO) of Memphis in May, says the real "meat" of the subject is ribs—dry, rub-covered, or wet—but ribs it is. Since I'm pretty sure I have eaten most of the best ribs I've ever had there, I've got to agree. But as I talk to restaurant owners, I'm equally certain that pulled and chopped pork shoulder is as much a staple there as it is across the rest of the state. And there are other elements—brisket is starting to creep its way in, no longer the property of more western varieties.

Tennessee barbecue, at its heart, comes of trying to make the best of a meal that might not be otherwise perfect—like the foods of the poor across the world, barbecue cooks of old learned to take their proteins and cook them slowly at low temperatures until the meat was fall-apart tender. Once they

mastered that, they found ways of making it better—mostly in the cooking process, in wood choice and temperature, and in smoke exposure.

And let's be honest, our Tennessee barbecue is not wholly unique—the cooking methods don't dramatically differ from the rest of the region, from Virginia and the Carolinas (though the sauces are often exceptionally different), from North Alabama and southern Kentucky, and the northwestern bits of Mississippi. Yet within our own culture, thanks to the rise of competition barbecue and the proliferation of the professional barbecue chef in part, we have notable points of difference.

In the African American communities in Memphis, you'll find sauce-heavy, succulent rib tips as a favorite meal, while at places like Charlie Vergos' Rendezvous, founded by the legendary Charlie Vergos, the thing is ribs with a combination of spices that blend Vergos's Greek ancestral tradition with the Cajun flavor palate he gleaned in New Orleans. These days, we think of those as Memphis-style ribs, and other restaurants have adapted the Vergos spice palate.

While pork is the dominant protein here and the pulled pork sandwich is de rigeur, chicken and turkey have their places, often dipped in rich, creamy

Alabama-style white sauce. Beef is finding its place, as the competition kings adopt the concepts from Kansas City and Texas and make it their own. Now, too, smoked sausages, bologna, and other incomers are slipping into the barbecue mainstream. Some of them have been part of the sadly less publicized African American barbecue scene all along and are finally getting due respect. Others we seem to have swiped from other regions and made our own. But if you ask for a smoked sausage and cheese plate in Memphis, you won't be disappointed either.

We've also hybridized a few foods—most notably, we love some barbecue nachos, a little barbecue spaghetti, or maybe a barbecue salad or pulled pork-topped baked potato. Some folks go as far as they can with it—a wood-fired barbecue pizza? No problem. And I hear rumor of the Nashville barbecue chefs adapting Kentucky mutton barbecue on occasion. Culture shifts, spreads, and brings delicious variances as we make it our own. In 20 years, who knows what else will be viewed as "Tennessee tradition"?

Our favorite side items remain as entrenched—coleslaw, mostly with a light mayonnaise, sometimes with vinegar or even mustard. In some places, especially the African American restaurants, this must always be on the sandwich; in others, it's optional (though just try to get past a Carey Bringle or a Pat Martin when you're skipping the coleslaw, I dare you). Baked beans and potato salad? Yes, please.

PHOTO COURTESY OF JOHN C. VERGOS AND RENDEZVOUS

At some restaurants, particularly along the back roads down here, that's all you'll find—pork sandwiches (in a purist, whole hog place, perhaps with no sauce at all), slaw, beans, potato salad, and maybe a dessert—probably banana pudding, fried pies, or a slice of cake. In Memphis, you might find a few butter cookies. That is the quintessence, the most essential part of barbecue. If you're in luck, the place you stop will offer you a cold Bud, but expect sweet tea, lemonade, and maybe a Coca-Cola.

The thing about so many of these little places is that they go in and out of business. That little place by the BP station on the corner might not be open the second time you go, then 2 years later it might have been taken over by someone else and reopened. It's a tough business that economically sometimes doesn't have much real reward. Many of the barbecue chefs you find here do have a love of the cooking.

Likewise, you won't find many rural holes in the wall in the literal sense listed in this book. It's too hard to collect them—and plenty of them are without identities on the Internet or even unreachable via phone. (My friend Martha Martin talks about the places her husband has taken her, where the guys in the pit have no shirts, and there's a sign saying "no smoking at the counter." Somehow, those manage to have the best food of all, the kind you remember.)

There's a place off exit 37 on I-65 as you head toward the Alabama border that sometimes has a portable shack and smoker out on weekends. I have absolutely no idea what it's called, and its appearance is as random as a door into Narnia, but man, it has good pork.

What you will find in this book is a collection of the best-known and the long-term barbecue places, the ones that might be there to welcome you as time passes. Some of them have been open for 20 years or more. And an astonishing number have been around fewer than 10, as barbecue culture really moved in and claimed its rightful place in cities like Nashville and Knoxville. I've included a short chapter on North Alabama because the border is an artificial thing, and there are a few places you need to visit if you find yourself there for business or pleasure—and if you watch the Food Network, you can't miss places like Big Bob Gibson's and Dreamland—as they're part of the cultural landscape. As with Tennessee, I encourage you to look for those little out-of-the-way places that look like they might fall apart over your ears and just go in and eat.

You'll also find a discussion of the barbecue festivals, a look at what a few home cooks I know are striving to do (and maybe see yourself in them), and a recipe collection of favorite items that, it is hoped, will help you with your next home barbecue. Some of them come from chefs like Carl Akins and Jason Little, who know barbecue but have passed their culinary time working everywhere from here in the MidSouth to New Orleans and the Midwest.

Most of the places in this book share in the fact that I or my friends personally enjoy them. I'm a bit biased that way. But for heaven's sake, if you're visiting Tennessee, take the time to get some good, local barbecue instead of hitting the mega-chain fast-food drive-through. You will not regret it. Heck, most of our barbecue joints have their own drive-through windows—they make you wait a bit longer than the golden arches, but it's worth it.

And I'll be honest—half the places in this book start with "try the pork sandwich." There's a reason for that—it's what we *do*, plain and simple. And done right, you just can't tire of good pulled pork.

A LITTLE HISTORY

While it may seem that writing about "Memphis" or "Tennessee" barbecue would be a very straightforward endeavor, it's actually rather complex. Depending on whom you ask on which street corner in which city, barbecue is a complex mélange of different things. Even within the city of Memphis and its environs, the definitions remain broad and mutable. While it's surely different than the heavily beef-dominated styles of Kansas City or Texas and the strong vinegar or mustard-sauced methods of North Carolina, you can't pin down the Memphis and Tennessee traditions to a single, easy definition. And that's as it should be. Behind that reality is a long history of traditional cooking, of farmers, and of a wide variety of cultures that made themselves a part of this region for more than 200 years.

Our Traditions

The MidSouth region is its own crossroads of sorts, lying between the midwestern influences of Missouri and Kansas and Virginia and the Carolinas to the south and east. Our barbecue sometimes draws in the flavors of other classic barbecue cooking territories—go to the right place in Memphis, and you'll find a sweet, heavy sauce reminiscent of Kansas City; hit the right spot in East Tennessee, and you'll get chopped barbecue (rather than pulled) with a vinegar heavy sauce or even a mustard-based one like the sort you find in South Carolina. Every now and then, you'll even find the smoky, capsaicin-dominant heat of a Texas-style sauce. Oh, and in Memphis, you'll find incredible ribs. Do not skip them.

But of course, we have our own thoughts about what makes up barbecue, including our take on sauces and dry rubs—but we'll come to that in a moment.

Our barbecue, like barbecue in those other regions, evolved over time from the need to use what meat was available, especially by the poorer and less privileged in society. Cooking a whole hog is difficult, as lifelong barbecue lovers and pitmasters will tell you. Pat Martin of Martin's Barbecue in Nolensville, Tennessee, will talk long and in incredible detail about what it takes to get shoulders and hams and bellies all cooked to the proper tenderness and temperature at the same time—it's no easy task. Zach Parker at Scott's-Parker's in West Tennessee is one of the few guys left in the state, heck, probably in the country, who is still dedicatedly smoking only whole hog, constantly displaying a dedication that astonishes and also begs us to find a way to preserve that tradition.

Sauces

Depending on where you are, sauces may be used to baste the meat, or they may appear on your table as an add-on component. Many barbecue places make their sauces in-house and have justifiable reason to be proud. In Tennessee, we tend toward dry rub with no sauce to begin, then use a wet mop (vinegar based) as the meat cooks to retain and maintain moisture. That varies pitmaster to pitmaster, of course—some add absolutely nothing, relying on proper cooking and the meat's own juices. Then we'll add a rub on the end in some cases. Some places choose to soak the barbecue in sauce before it's served, especially ribs—but that's far from all of them.

BIG BOB GIBSON'S

Alabama White Sauce—A tangy, often peppery sauce in a mayonnaise base. Alabama white is most associated with Big Bob Gibson's Decatur, Alabama, restaurants dating back to the 1920s. Generally a condiment for smoked chicken and turkey but also used on other proteins.

Carolina "Gold"—A tangy, spicy, mustard-based sauce popular in the Carolinas and East Tennessee.

Dry Rub—A mix of herbs and spices, often combined with salt or sugar applied to the meat before cooking or immediately afterward to impart flavor and to seal in moisture. Memphis-style barbecue, especially ribs, often depends on the use of a dry rub, but they are common throughout the region.

"Hot" Sauce—Typically a tomato puree or ketchup-based sauce with vinegar and a little sweetener, to which chili powder, jalapeños, habañero, or other peppers have been added. If you aren't a fan of true heat, always taste the sauce before you liberally dowse your sandwich. Sometimes you'll see a sauce labeled "Sweet Heat" or some variation thereof—note that sweet does not negate heat, and try before you apply.

Kansas City Style—A thick, sweeter sauce making use of molasses, corn syrup or honey, and brown sugar. Typically, it's in a tomato base, with vinegar and spices. It tends to be heavier and sweeter than many Tennessee-style sauces.

Memphis Style—A lighter alternative to the Kansas City tradition, it's tomato based with some vinegar and usually a sweetening and thickening agent, such as a bit of molasses or brown sugar, plus herbs and spices.

"Mild" Sauce—In Tennessee, this tends toward a ketchup base with vinegar and a little sugar or sweetener, plus fairly mild spices—enough for a tang but not real heat.

North Carolina Style—A heavily vinegar-based sauce, thinner, and often used as a "mop" during cooking in other barbecue traditions. Some variations use red pepper flake and black pepper to give it some heat. Many also add a bit of tomato puree, especially for applying after cooking. It may also be called just "Carolina" or even "South Carolina" style.

Texas Style—The Kansas City sweetening tradition has crept into the Texas variety as well, but old-school Texas sauce blends vinegar with heat-heavy spices—pepper, onion, chilis, cumin, other peppers, vinegar. and a bit of tomato. In some cases, Texas sauces utilize meat dripping, giving them a smoky flavor on the palate.

Barbecue as we know it probably came from slaves and from the poor cooking hogs, trying to get tough old meat to turn into something not only hearty and filling but truly good as well. It wasn't so much originally the food of the moneyed, who could afford the most tender roasts on their white linen tablecloths and china serving plates. And a pig is an animal where you can find something good to eat on the whole thing—a ham hock to flavor your beans, perhaps, or still-popular chitterlings. And even the skin, prized for its rich, crunchy texture, becomes part of the meal. There are cooks and foodies who value a good piece of crispy skin more than anything. If you've never pulled a piece of hot skin off a newly roasted pig, burning your fingers and almost burning your mouth, you've missed something. (Yeah, they sell pork rinds in the Kroger, but nothing is the same as fresh from the smoker or the spit—nothing.)

Time & Again

Over the years—by which I mean centuries—barbecue truly became the food of farmers and rural dwellers, those who lived close to the land. It was a generational thing, with the skills of the barbecue pitmaster often passed down from generation to generation.

Some people will earnestly tell you that "Tennessee" barbecue *absolutely* requires pork, but when you ask whether that's whole hog, ribs, shoulders, or butts, the debate engages—and do you pull that pork or chop it?

At this stage of the game, all those variations are in play, even in the parts of the state where one particular type has held sway for decades. Times change, people share knowledge, and the competition circuit has opened everyone up to new ideas. Heck, given its level of publicity, the competition circuit has probably been the reason you now find Tennessee-style barbecue joints in Brooklyn, Los Angeles, and Detroit.

Then the crucial cooking issues come along to debate—dry rub? With what, and before or after? Are you cooking in a pit or with a smoker—and, if so, is that starting and finishing and with wood or charcoal? The answer to all these questions is yes.

The ultimate in old-school Tennessee barbecue, especially in West Tennessee at least up until a decade ago, was the previously mentioned whole hog—but even that has caveats; the trends and traditions have shifted strongly over the years.

Meanwhile, the big barbecue circuit changed our views and methodologies, and pitmasters of newer immigrant stock brought their own families' traditions into it all—as with Charlie Vergos' Rendezvous in Memphis, where the dry rub and rib traditions really took off. The Rendezvous dry rub comes from a blend of the traditional herbs and spices that Vergos's Greek family used for lamb and the influence of Cajun spices from his own visits to New Orleans. Yet now, they're nearly synonymous with Memphis-style ribs and Tennessee-style barbecue.

The pulled pork sandwich is ubiquitous—everyone has one, and for many restaurants, it remains the specialty of the house—the thing you want to order without thinking the first time you come in—and maybe the fifth or the 25th. The pork may be served up on a classic white bun, corn bread (especially in Middle Tennessee), or lately on top of a baked potato, nachos, spaghetti, or heaven help us, a salad. The important part is that it's slow-cooked pork.

And of course, as you move out, you find that the Tennessee idea of barbecue also sees close parallels in North Alabama, southern Kentucky, and even northern Mississippi and west Arkansas. This is an interrelated culture, and if you talk to people like *Tennessean* food critic Jim Myers, he'll argue vociferously that a lot of Tennessee barbecue culture is Alabama barbecue culture too. It's a chicken-and-egg debate. Borders be damned, this is regional food, larger than a state line.

And you discover that proteins these days are negotiable. While pork is surely dominant, some of the state's very best barbecue, from Memphis across the midstate and into the Smoky Mountains, includes chicken, turkey, sausage, bologna, beef brisket, and, in some cases, mutton or lamb (this last especially in western Kentucky).

Likewise, since the advent of that barbecue circuit, combined with a fluid society in which people pick up and move across regions so often, many of the popular styles from those other places have bled into ours. Restaurants serving good Texas or Carolina style set up in our metropolitan areas and find their place in the firmament. We cross-pollinate, adding to our tradition. Because of that, I've included some very good restaurants in this book where the owners consider their style "more Kansas City" or "kind of Carolina."

While that may confuse you a little, what it underlines is that Tennessee is very serious about its barbecue, and the state is willing to have an inner debate about what's best. You can likely find examples of all of it at the big barbecue festivals that hugely impact the state's tourism dollars, including Memphis in May and the Jack Daniel's World Championship Invitational Barbecue in Lynchburg. (And practically all of them use the Kansas City Barbecue Society's set of judging rules—though you'll find some fixed to the Memphis Barbecue Network and a few small spots that just judge on taste, rules be damned.)

Regions & Favorites, From Shoulders to Whole Hog

A serious aficionado could take a year or so and just drive the state, starting at either end, and explore the best barbecue on offer. Some of it will come from the famous outlets in Memphis, from Jim Neely's Interstate and Charlie Vergos' Rendezvous and their ilk. Some will come from the wilds of East Tennessee, from Ridgewood in Bluff City, nearly in Virginia, and from Dead End or Sweet P's in Knoxville. Middle Tennessee offers up its younger legends—like Pat Martin and Carey Bringle, who have moved Nashville at last away from the world of endless chains, and Edley's, with its Birmingham and rural McMinnville, Tennessee, influences. And along the way, in between major cities, you'll find some of the best barbecue coming from tiny stops along the interstate and state highways in out-of-the-way places you never would have expected.

Indeed, driving the back roads of Tennessee reveals those little shacks and gas stations where someone has a smoker out back, cooking up something fantastic, toothsome, and wonderful—pork smoked just right over hickory so that the cartilage has melted and the flavor is deep, perhaps with crispy bits of skin mixed in (something you find a lot with whole hog). And make no mistake—some of the least impressive buildings may lead to the most flavorful and delicious barbecue. I've made note of a few for you.

Especially in the counties in West Tennessee an hour or so outside Memphis, whole hog used to be king. Back in the day, farmers supplemented their incomes by working all week, then Thursday or Friday would get together friends and cook up a hog. They'd open up Friday, Saturday, and Sunday—or until the meat was gone—and sell barbecue. It might come with coleslaw and a side or two—beans, mac and cheese, corn bread, plus a dessert made by wives and daughters. Whole hog was usually a man's game—a way of socializing as much as of cooking.

These days, as the experts like Nick Pihakis, Chris Chamberlain, or Thomas Williams will tell you, that kind of West Tennessee whole hog practice no longer truly exists on any kind of scale. A lot of people mourn that as a tragic loss, but the economics of it make for a ready explanation: shoulders and butts can be cheaper and are far easier to cook than whole hog. Sons moved away and gave up their fathers' dedication to weekends spent smoking a hog, then selling pulled pork for the weekend until it ran out, supplementing their farm income. And as prices changed and the processing plants moved or closed, it no longer really paid you back for work, time, and investment.

And that's one reason that much of West Tennessee now offers smoked shoulders and butts instead—it is less labor intensive and provides a better profit margin. It makes sense, as it's still delicious, but you have to hope, like Pat Martin says, that we don't lose the art and prowess in the process. Although a number of pitmasters—often urban today—dedicate themselves to reviving the style on the back roads and in the country, it's simply gone almost everywhere.

Pihakis, founder of Birmingham, Alabama–based Jim N' Nick's, one of the few barbecue chains that seems to remain true to the region and to its sense of flavor, has dedicated the past 30 years to making good barbecue happen. He's one of the founders of the Fatback Pig Project, aiming to make growing hogs a viable farming profession again.

With the aid of people like the consortium he helped form at the Fatback Pig Project, he's not only encouraging the reopening of true family hog farming in regional agriculture but also bringing about a return to the use of heritage hogs for some of the major chefs and pitmasters in the region. Part of that has to do with the opening of Fatback's new hog processing facility near Cullman, Alabama (about 2½ hours south of Nashville on I-65)—because there hadn't been one in the region for years.

The goal is not only to restore both heritage and commercial hog farming and make processing accessible here but also to help bring down the price of locally farmed animals. This is an era when hormone-heavy, factory-farmed animals are cheapest and when families of all income brackets would like to break those ties to factory farms but sometimes find the higher prices impossible for their budgets.

Wherever you are in the state, you'll find a discussion about pork and beef prices. There's no question they're rising, especially when you talk about beef brisket. That has a lot to do with the ongoing decade of drought across Texas and Oklahoma that has shrunk cattle herds in its wake. And brisket, once favored because it was a cheap cut of beef, is now so popular that prices have gone up to reflect that. But in the case of both cattle and hogs, there are plenty of farmers who simply realized the economic benefit of just growing corn for the ever-increasing market rather than keeping their cows and pigs as primary moneymakers.

Patrick Martin, a Middle Tennessee pitmaster who has become something of a legend thanks to his appearances on the Food Network and at Big Apple Barbecue in New York, exemplifies what it means to be a barbecue chef with a tradition behind you in Tennessee. Born just south of Memphis in Mississippi and educated in West Tennessee, Martin says his family originally came to northern Mississippi from the Carolinas, bringing with them that territory's flavor profiles. His story is not unlike many others in his position, though they may lack the professional credentials Martin has now garnered.

Proteins

One of the things that distinguishes Tennessee barbecue is slow cooking to break down the meat proteins, often with a dry rub and a wet mop of a vinegar mixture to maintain moisture. While pork is king in the region, expect other proteins to show up on your menu.

Pork Shoulder and Pork Butt—These are the absolute staple of the barbecue world in Tennessee. Here, you'll find that most are slow smoked for hours over wood or charcoal, depending on the pitmaster's tastes, and then let to rest for hours more, until the meat almost falls apart and is easily pulled. The chopped meat style is more traditional in Carolina barbecue and the sliced meat in Texas, but occasionally you'll see both here.

Whole Hog—Once the heart of West Tennessee and some Middle Tennessee and North Alabama traditions, whole hog is truly rare now given the lack of suppliers. You'll still find some old-school, rural West Tennessee guys (often farmers) who have their pits going on weekends and who sell until the meat is gone, but over the years, many of them—or their children—have turned toward shoulders and butts, which are easier and more profitable overall than whole hog. Some chefs have recently tried to restore whole hog cooking to its place in the barbecue firmament, including Pat Martin and Cary Bringle in Nashville. In West Tennessee, the best source is Scott's-Parker's Barbecue with pitmaster Zach Parker, who does nothing but whole hog.

Pork Ribs—Charlie Vergos started grilling ribs in his restaurant in the early 1950s and defined them as a Memphis barbecue staple where pulled pork had once been the dominant form. He coated them with a seasoning blend combining the herbs and spices of his Greek heritage with the Cajun seasonings he'd found in New Orleans, and the dry rub concept was born. Ribs from Charlie Vergos' Rendezvous are still one of the most sought-after barbecue meals in the state, and ribs have become synonymous with Memphis style.

Rib Tips—A staple in the African American community in Memphis particularly, this is some tender pork cooked to perfection and usually served up thick and heavy with a Memphis-style sweet or sweet-hot sauce on a soft bun. Look for them especially at places like A&R and Jim Neely's Interstate.

Chicken—Popular with competition barbecue teams, barbecue chicken is almost as much a staple as pork in Tennessee these days. In North Alabama, Big Bob Gibson's tangy white sauce made chicken a formidable part of the barbecue culture, and white sauces are now made throughout the region.

Brisket—Beef brisket, served sliced, has a much closer association with Texas and Kansas City than Tennessee, but many of the barbecue restaurants in the region include it on regular menus these days. The growing popularity of beef in the big barbecue competitions certainly plays into its proliferation.

Mutton and Lamb—Staples of barbecue in Kentucky, especially in the western part of the state (thanks to wool production dating back close to 200 years), they sometimes show up on barbecue menus in Tennessee as well. Expect mutton to also be slow cooked to break down the tough meat, treated with dry rub, and wet mopped with a vinegar mixture, with a table sauce of some kind in many places.

Sausage—Both Memphis and Middle Tennessee had a large influx of German immigrants, and smoked sausage—often served as a starter at larger barbecue restaurants, with cheese (sometimes also smoked) and bread or crackers—remains a popular barbecue protein.

Bologna—This is not the stuff you get prepackaged at the supermarket—sandwiches featuring thick slices of smoked bologna are popping up across the state. The origins of "barbecue" bologna are a little foggy—both Oklahoma and West Virginia make claims for its origins, and you'll find recipes for it calling it things like "Mississippi prime rib," but regardless of where it first started, it's a frequent addition to the barbecue repertoire in the state of Tennessee.

Tennessee's barbecue culture is thriving. The conversation has been informed by the old traditions of West Tennessee whole hog, Memphis's ribs, the pulled pork butts and shoulders that have long since become the norm across the state, and the additions of other proteins through either contact with other regions or the resurgence of old interest. Add to that the barbecue festival circuit as codified and exemplified by the Kansas City Barbecue Society and the Memphis Barbecue Network, and a defining moment for good food is born.

This book is divided by region, though the styles of those regions overlap—you can find Alabama white sauce in Middle Tennessee, West Tennessee whole hog in North Alabama, and Memphis dry rub ribs in East Tennessee: multitudes of examples of cultural sharing across the state and beyond.

Nashville's Carey Bringle of Peg Leg Porker exemplifies the way that Tennessee's barbecue evangelism moves across the state. Born in Memphis but raised largely in Nashville, he learned his skills helping his family members cook, and he brings to the business his memories of barbecue joints in Memphis that he visited with parents and grandparents on regular return visits to the area. His place in Nashville's rapidly expanding Gulch neighborhood, with its simple, straightforward menu; its concrete floors; and its vibrant collection of family photos blown up on the walls, is a paean to all his formative Memphis barbecue experience. The food celebrates everything from Memphis dry rub ribs to the ubiquitous pulled pork sandwich to the newer hybrids, like barbecue nachos. (Get the ribs on your first visit—with smoked green beans.) These days, he's also working on a proprietary house bourbon.

George Ewart at Dead End in Knoxville took an alternative route to becoming a serious pitmaster—like Bringle and Martin, he grew up cooking barbecue with family members. Around 2002, he found himself cooking a whole hog as a one-off for a neighborhood Memorial Day celebration, and as a result, he soon found himself smack in the middle of the competition barbecue circuit—not so uncommon here. Before he knew it, he was opening a restaurant and turning all the combined knowledge gained from family tradition and competition into a barbecue philosophy that helps define Knoxville's place in the Tennessee barbecue world.

In tiny Woodbury, Tennessee, between Murfreesboro and McMinnville, you find guys like Mike Alexander who get into barbecue as a hobby—and soon they have a catering gig or two and then a food truck and still maintain a day job. With no direct plans to open a brick and mortar yet, Mike exemplifies the folks who just can't quit their love for barbecue. Mike and his crew travel all over Middle and East Tennessee, catering or selling directly from their distinctive food truck—from Pulaski on the Alabama border to Lookout Mountain just shy of Georgia. This stretch of Tennessee is notably lacking in locally owned restaurants, and it's the barbecue guys, including folks like Mike, who help keep local flavors alive and thriving in a realm of fast-food drive-throughs and midrange sit-down, generic chains.

Out in West Tennessee, Helen Turner proves that a female pitmaster is a formidable being, and she cooks up shoulders and serves them with no need for seasonings—just perfectly smoked pork from her pits, the way it was intended to be at its most fundamental. That Helen is a joy to talk to and a power house all her own only adds to her legend in the world of Tennessee barbecue cooking.

In Memphis, Jim Neely has spent 30 years defining an ideal for Memphis barbecue, and there the African American community remains strong and ever present in the Tennessee barbecue universe. That collection of outstanding barbecuers represents long family traditions in this branch of the culinary world, a deep and marvelous contrast and inspiration to latecomers inspired by competition barbecue. Yet all the styles and joints in town blend together so well, creating an environment of good food served up by good people, regardless of which one you walk into, from prominent places like Jim Neely's Interstate, Memphis Barbecue Co., and Charlie Vergos' Rendezvous to smaller places like A&R Barbecue and The Bar-B-Q Shop.

Tennessee style is itself a hybrid—it brings together the centuries-old history of the poor, both urban and rural, making the best of tough meats, and then blends in the cooking traditions of its own region and several beyond. Today as in the past, you can find a good joint nearly everywhere along the highways and byways, and you can also visit big-name barbecue legends built on festival publicity. Pitmasters have become celebrities of sorts. And everywhere you go, there's a good sandwich waiting for you to find it.

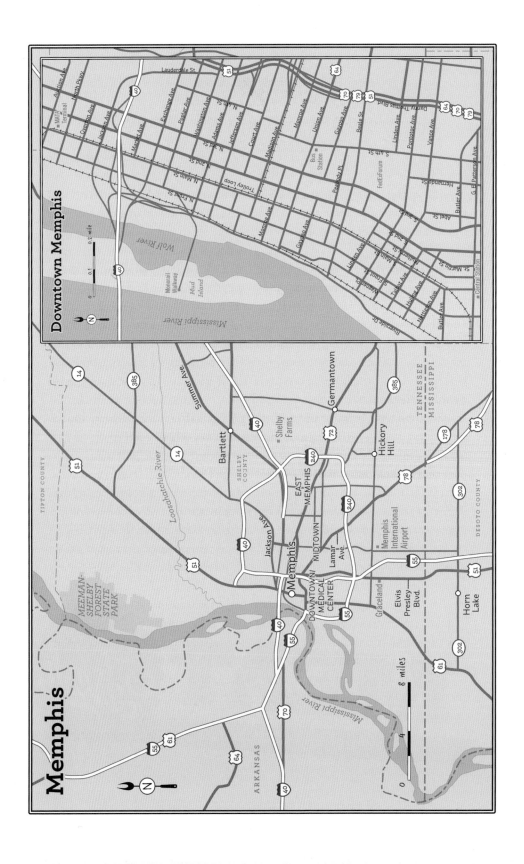

Memphis

Memphis residents were a little surprised to recently discover that Nashville had been proclaimed barbecue capital of the US by assorted media outlets. Now, I've got nothing bad to say about the part of the state I live in, but in terms of good restaurants per capita, I think Memphis is still the winner. I can behold good barbecue on every single corner and in every last nook and cranny of this city. Some of those places, many covered in this book, have gotten much-deserved national recognition. Others remain unknown to anyone outside the neighborhood they inhabit. It goes without saying that while every now and then you're going to find that one experience that might somehow disappoint (because they happen), most of the options in the city are going to leave you pleased.

Memphis style is many and varied—*styles*, plural, might be a better way of putting it. Like most of the rest of this region, they smoke their proteins, but just how that gets done varies—some chefs swear by premade charcoal with perhaps a little hickory to finish, some vow they use nothing but the woods themselves, and others use newer technology: gas-fired or electric smokers and the like with wood for flavor purposes. But what we know, regardless of the methodology, is that Memphis restaurants consistently produce outstanding, tender, juicy meats that have gained them a reputation over the years. There is valid reason for people to think that Tennessee and Memphis styles are synonymous because Memphis made its name first.

Beyond cooking methodology, there are sauce and seasoning traditions we take for granted, even though they come from a variety of cultural origins, some very recent. Charlie Vergos' Rendezvous cooks up the epitome of the Memphis-style ribs, delicious in every way, but the Vergos family readily acknowledges that the dry rub they're famous for traces back to Vergos's own Greek roots and the influence of Cajun seasoning garnered on trips to Louisiana.

Some of the oldest Memphis barbecue traditions tie back to the African American community in the city, and many of today's professional chefs (a group in which I include a plethora of Caucasians as well) have childhood memories of tiny street-corner joints run by fantastically gifted African American chefs in turn who brought their own perspectives to the barbecue world. Some of those can still be seen (and tasted) at places like A&R and Cozy Corner. And those places tend toward thick, decidedly sweet sauces with molasses and tomato, tangy with a hint of spice—unless you pick up the sauce that says "hot."

And, of course, the competition barbecue circuit plays into all of it as well, with serious winning competitors—for example, Melissa Cookston at Memphis Barbecue Co.—bringing in perspectives learned from years cooking for judges and winning.

That the Memphis in May International Festival sponsors one of the biggest, best, and most wonderful of barbecue competitions in the world there each year just encourages tourists, barbecue lovers, and chefs alike to flood into the city and cook—or eat—like mad for days. And when they're not at the festival, those barbecue chefs and aficionados can be found exploring the places nearby—the joints run by the guys who are happy to cook for you, even if competing isn't their thing.

All of this plays into what makes Memphis barbecue. In spite of the fact that every single place has a pork sandwich, they're rarely the same—the nuances of methodology make sure of that. Still, they're part of what I consider true Tennessee barbecue, whether they're dripping sauce and coleslaw, slathered with the spices of a dry rub, or just pure meat served up for us to appreciate the cooking skill.

My first real trip to Memphis to eat, I have to admit, was really to meet up with my new boyfriend (now my husband) Seth and some friends for a weekend, several of whom had driven up from Baton Rouge. Because we were all staying at a hotel, we took the advice of local friends and made our way to a rather unprepossessing barbecue place, at least from the looks of it, where the ribs turned out to be as big as our heads and incredibly delicious. My friend Lara Olstad and I to this day joke about "brontosaurus ribs" that we watched the guys demolish while we delicately tried to eat our pork sandwiches.

I've never managed to find that place again—it may have closed or moved, or I just may be confused about the name—but it came to be the symbol for me of what to expect in Memphis—the city rarely disappoints when cooking pork shoulder or butts and ribs is concerned. Memphis is a glorious culinary experience everyone should have occasionally. And if your idea of culinary escape involves a big wine and cocktail list and elegant tablecloths, it's time to let go, eat with your fingers, and be a little sloppy.

Although the following collection of restaurants is far from absolute and definitive, it makes for a very good place to start.

A&R Bar-B-Que

3721 Hickory Hill Rd., East Memphis, TN 38106, (901) 365-9777; 1802 Elvis Presley Blvd., Memphis, TN 38115 (Whitehaven), (901) 774-7444; aandrbbq.com

Lashun Pollard Tate's father Andrew opened A&R in 1983 together with his wife, Rose—the A and R of the restaurant's name. Andrew Pollard had always dreamed of opening a barbecue restaurant, and when the meatpacking plant he had worked at for 19 years closed, he saw the opportunity and took it. With him, he brought an exceptional knowledge of meats. Today, he's mostly retired for health reasons, and his daughter Lashun and son Brian operate the two locations.

"We're completely family owned and operated," says Tate. "We have been from the beginning; my dad made a point to employ family members who needed or wanted it. We take care of each other and believe in giving back to the community—we have a very Christ-centered perspective." Over the years, they've won a huge number of accolades for their wonderful home-style comfort food and have been featured in a plethora of magazines and television shows.

The restaurants, which showcase the deep and wonderful African American barbecue tradition in Memphis, started with pork, ribs, and rib tips cooked over hickory charcoal and wood chips. The restaurant reflects the African American take on Memphis style, with barbecue bologna and rib tips being menu favorites and meats served up "sloppy," in Tate's words, with the delicious, sweet and tangy house sauce "dripping off the meat." Expect to get coleslaw on your sandwich unless you request otherwise. Bottled beer can be ordered as well as tea and soft drinks.

On your visit, try the rib tip sandwich or the rib tips and fries to understand why the rib tips are in such great demand. The ribs themselves and the pork sandwich remain popular too. On the side, try the baked beans and the coleslaw made from Rose Pollard's own recipe. Absolutely save room for fried pies—if you're not from the South, you won't get it until you've tried one—and these are fantastic. Or you can choose lemon, caramel, or chocolate cake and a variety of regular pie, peach cobbler, and house-made butter cookies that are a Memphis favorite. Catering and private banquet room facilities are available.

The Bar-B-Q Shop

1782 Madison Ave, Memphis, TN 38104; (901) 272-1277; dancingpigs .com

Eric Vernon has an MBA in marketing, which means he could have made plenty of different life choices. But when it came down to it, he couldn't walk away from his family's barbecue business. That's a good thing because the Bar-B-Q Shop has a long history, beginning with a trained chef, Mr. Brady Vincent, who lived above his barbecue restaurant for many years and truly is the originator of barbecue spaghetti. In the early 1980s, "Mr. Brady," as folks called him, began talking about retirement, and Frank and Hazelteen Vernon, Eric's parents—regular patrons and former restaurant owners—worked out a deal to buy the restaurant.

"Mr. Brady lived above the restaurant, and every day for a year, he came downstairs in the morning and taught my mother to make everything from scratch the way he did." Eric, their son, maintains the traditions.

Meats are cooked over charcoal and hickory wood. The barbecue spaghetti, which may look like just sauce and noodles, remains a slow, intricate process, with a base that cooks slowly for 12 solid hours before cooling and adding to the noodles. "It's a little sweet, a little oily, with a smoky flavor. It's something you can't get from just pouring a sauce on," says Eric.

Besides the spaghetti, order the barbecue sandwich on Texas toast, either chopped or pulled. Don't forget house-made coleslaw. The barbecue bologna, smoked in the pit, has plenty of fans too. "And we have incredible fries," says Eric. "And beer battered onion rings." The barbecue salad here is worth the order as well.

To drink, there's beer, or get soda and house-made sweet tea. You can buy the famous sauce and rubs to go, in the restaurant and on the website, as well as at Kroger around the region. Those dancing pigs holding hands on the label are a happy throwback reference to the days of Mr. and Mrs. Brady Vincent, by the way. Closed Sunday.

Big Bill's BBQ

4101 Elvis Presley Blvd., Memphis, TN 38116; (901) 552-4502

If you find yourself somewhere near Graceland and want to grab some barbecue, this small joint is very likely to please. It's a small, mid-century style of outfit set in the midst of a strip center, but, as we know, Tennessee barbecue is often at its best when it's not in some fancy space. The menu and food stylings lean to African American tradition, meaning that you can expect plenty of really good sauce (mild or spicy) dripping from your sandwich. The restaurant is usually busy with customers, and the atmosphere couldn't be more welcoming. Look for shiny red vinyl booths and a vibe that could as easily belong in 1965 as the present.

The ribs and the rib tips are definitely on the must-order list. Expect them truly saucy unless you request otherwise, but take a few wet wipes along for the experience. The pork sandwich (chopped) is also an excellent option. Don't be surprised if that sauce has spilled over onto your fries, but that's okay—it's delicious there as well.

Big Bill's is the kind of under-the-radar, off-the-beaten-path place you want to try instead of the many chains that dominate this part of the city. If you're a fan of hot sauce, apply it liberally here—it won't burn your mouth, but it has a really pleasant heat if you like some spice on your barbecue without its being overwhelming.

There's brisket as well as pork if you're of a mind for beef, and Big Bill's seems to give it more attention than the average in Memphis, where pork dominates. This is another spot where you should expect the coleslaw to be served on your sandwich unless you ask for it otherwise. Portions are generous and prices moderate. Closed Sunday.

Blues City Café

138 Beale St., Memphis, TN 38103; (901) 526-3637; bluescitycafe.com

It says a lot for Blues City that I can shoot the breeze there with waiters like Edgar Smith, who've been there since the restaurant opened in 1992. Mind you, it started as a franchise of the famous Doe's Eat Place in Greenville, Mississippi, which spent all its time focused on making a good steak. That's all well and good, but by 1993, the Memphis franchisees had separated and renamed the place, and in 1994, with the help of the late chef, Mr. Bonnie Mack, they turned the focus to ribs. Since then, Blues City Café has attracted a plethora of big-name visitors, from Robert Duvall to Al Green (who used an image of the restaurant's front as an album cover). Parts of the movie *The Firm* were shot here, and Bobby Flay has promoted it on the Food Network.

Set right on Beale Street, the restaurant is frequently crowded, and they come for the ribs. These ribs, baby back pork from young, tender pigs, are cooked over hickory and served up wet, using a Memphis-style sauce heavy on molasses and brown sugar. (You can find the sauce and the rubs for sale on the website listed above.)

On the side, expect standards like French fries, coleslaw, and baked beans. You can order sandwiches during the day, including a barbecue pork po'boy, but not at night. But whenever you go in, just order up the ribs. The only meat they cook barbecue style is pork, so while there are other proteins on the menu, if it's barbecue you're wanting, be aware.

One thing you'll discover here is a good mix of the tourists who've come for the atmosphere and locals who've come in because they want to eat. The fact that Blues City has a full bar clearly doesn't hurt in attracting both.

Central Barbecue

2249 Central Ave., Memphis, TN 38104, (901) 272-9377; 4375 Summer Ave., Memphis, TN 38122, (901) 767-4672; 147 E. Butler Ave., Memphis, TN 38103, (901) 672-7760; cbqmemphis.com

Craig Blondis and Roger Sapp created Central Barbecue in 2003 after years of defining their skill as pitmasters on competition teams (separate teams, in fact), including at Memphis in May. "We brought competitive style to the restaurant business," says Blondis. Between the two of them, they've accumulated more than 40 years' worth of competition experience, and they aim to share what they've learned.

Blondis says that the philosophy at Central means dry—a rub, marinating the meat thoroughly overnight, then slow cooking it with no sauce at all. They make use of hickory and pecan wood in their smokers (for flavor, with the heat coming from charcoal compared to gas in the restaurant) to give the meat the perfect wood flavor. "It's the wood that defines Tennessee barbecue," asserts Blondis, referencing the use of hickory and sometimes pecan that's so prevalent in this part of the country.

The competition viewpoint of Central means that sauce is a secondary thing, not a means to an end, so consider it a condiment here. They still make the vinegar- and mustard-based sauces in-house but outsource the recipes (with no harm done to flavor) of the mild and hot sauces to a company in nearby Hernando, Mississippi. The mild is Memphis style, with molasses, brown sugar, and lots of tomato, while the hot is a heady mix of bourbon and Tabasco tastes.

Order ribs or the pulled pork to begin: They're mostly cooking shoulders, but once in a while, they'll do some small whole hog and have a little "pig pickin'" for a special occasion or weekend. There's quite a list of proteins: the almost de rigeur Memphis smoked bologna done very right, turkey breast, pulled and half chickens, and beef brisket.

The smoked hot wings make a terrific starter, as do the barbecued nachos, a mix of fresh chips, shredded cheese, meat, jalapeños, meat, sauce, and a shake of seasoning.

You won't lack for classic sides like slaw, potato salad, and beans, but the house-made pork rinds and potato chips are seriously flavorful selections. Blondis really recommends the potato chips. And if you need a beer to wash it all down with, there's plenty of local and regional stuff to quaff. From Nashville's Yazoo and St. Louis's Schlafly and four different Memphis brews, they have you covered.

And your visit? "It's the same experience you'd have if you were a judge at a barbecue contest," says Blondis. Catering available.

Charlie Vergos' Rendezvous
52 S. Second St., Memphis, TN 38103; (901) 523-2746; hogsfly.com

The power house that is Charlie Vergos' Rendezvous can claim responsibility to a great extent for what we think of as "Memphis" barbecue. Back in 1948, Charlie Vergos opened a restaurant with his brother-in-law. It didn't bring in enough to support two families, so Charlie opted to clean out the basement, deck it out in a wild collection of materials bought up and down the street from local merchants, and open up an 80-seat tavern. In the 1950s, he cleared out the old coal chutes and started grilling. His specialty was ribs—something you didn't see in barbecue places at all at the time, seasoned with a combination of

his family's traditional Greek lamb seasonings and the Cajun-style spices he had recently discovered on a visit to New Orleans. The results are now synonymous with Memphis style.

Charlie passed away in 2010, but sons John and Nick still operate the now 700-seat restaurant, set in an alley a stone's throw from the celebrated Peabody Hotel. Over the years, they've served everyone from politicians to the Rolling Stones (who've also jammed at the restaurant—you never know who will turn up).

Needless to say, when you visit, plan on ordering the ribs because not to do so would be a shame. They don't come slathered in sauce, but they don't need it (sauce is on the table if you require it). You can absolutely order a pork shoulder or chicken sandwich, and make sure to start with an appetizer plate of sausage and cheese. If you're not a big meat eater, there's a killer Greek salad featuring a family recipe for Greek dressing and some vegetarian red beans and rice.

You can order Vergos' famous seasoning and house sauces online at the restaurant's website. You can also get ribs shipped by FedEx if you can't travel and want to try them, courtesy of the restaurant's USDA-certified kitchen.

The Chains: Corky's Ribs & BBQ

Corky's (corkysribsandbarbecue.com) was one of my first exposures to chain barbecue in Middle Tennessee, specifically the franchise on Franklin Road in Brentwood—a welcome alternative to the standard chain fast-food fare, as many barbecue franchises in Tennessee prove to be for folks tired of the same old hamburgers and chicken fingers. But the truth is, Corky's has its home in Memphis, where you can still find the original restaurant and several iterations of the chain.

The chain version Corky's is a franchise of the original Memphis restaurant, founded by barbecue restaurant veteran Don Pelts in 1984 in East Memphis—which still exists and is well worth its own excursion. Corky's was one of the first well-known Memphis barbecue locations to pursue the takeout/drive-through zeitgeist of the 1980s and did it very successfully. Many of the franchises also offer catering for events and parties as well as the drive-through and sit-down portion of the restaurant business.

Look for pulled pork, beef brisket, chicken, and turkey on the menu, but there's also a lot of fun in the fact that you can get ribs through a drive-up window—both dry rub and soaked in the restaurant's signature sauce. There are solid sides available, and the pies are pretty good too.

Of note, like many of the good Memphis places, Corky's allows you to order your ribs, and they'll ship by FedEx to any place in the country. If you're planning to order a Memphis snack online or by phone, you might really appreciate some of Corky's ribs delivered to your door.

Memphis Travel

Of course, when you're in Memphis, quite aside from Memphis in May, there are a few spots you won't want to miss.

Graceland (3734 Elvis Presley Blvd., Memphis, TN 38116; graceland.com)—For decades, fans of the King who listened back then and who weren't even born when he passed away have made pilgrimages to his gorgeous Memphis home. It's been immortalized in movies, on television, and in songs. If you go to Memphis, you've got to make the trip—and plenty of good barbecue joints are nearby. To quote Paul Simon, "I've reason to believe, we all will be received in Graceland."

Memphis Brooks Museum of Art (1934 Poplar Ave., Memphis, TN 38104; brooksmuseum.org)—Dating back to 1916, the Brooks Museum is one of the oldest in Tennessee, with a fine American art collection, including late 19th- and early 20th-century artists of note Cecilia Beaux, Edward Redfield, and William Merritt Chase and an impressive Old Masters collection, plus a variety of excellent touring exhibitions.

National Civil Rights Museum at the Lorraine Motel (450 Mulberry St., Memphis, TN 38103; civilrightsmuseum.org)—A privately owned museum complex paying tribute to the civil rights movement, guaranteed to move your heart. It's a valuable, teachable American history experience telling the story of the civil rights movement and its heroes, including the Rev. Martin Luther King Jr.

The Peabody Hotel (peabodymemphis.com)—The elegant Peabody in downtown Memphis is the favorite place to stay. It's close by any number of major attractions, music venues, and downtown restaurants, but the favorite aspect is usually the Peabody ducks. For some 80 years, the Peabody ducks—once live duck decoys—have paraded through the lobby each day to swim in the fountain, trained by the hotel's resident duck master. You won't find duck on the hotel restaurant's menu, but you'll love the site of the daily duck parade, and this is a great place to make a reservation for your visit.

(continued)

Stax Museum of American Soul Music (926 E. McLemore Ave., Memphis, TN 38106; staxmuseum.com)—Located at the original home of the little record store that started it all, the Stax Museum tells the story of soul music in the US and pays tribute to its artists, with more than 2,000 interactive exhibits. A must for music lovers everywhere.

Sun Studios (sunstudio.com/plan-your-tour)—Visit the home of the original Sun Records, where Elvis did much of his early recording, as did Johnny Cash, Jerry Lee Lewis, Carl Perkins, and a host of other major names in the history of rock-and-roll music. The site is only about 15 minutes from Graceland, so plan to visit on the same day.

This place is legendary for its food, the celebrities who make sure to eat there, and a staff that doesn't turn over (they have more than 30 employees with 25 years or more of experience, thanks to good pay, benefits, sick days, and vacation time that the Vergos family is proud to provide). Closed on Sunday and Monday.

Cozy Corner

745 North Pkwy., Memphis, TN 38105; (901) 527-9158; cozycorner.com
Plenty of folks still swear by Cozy Corner and think it's the best thing in town, though it's been around for decades. In fact, I know people who make a point of visiting every time they're in Memphis, which speaks to just how good this place remains. It's now in the hands of Desiree Robinson, wife of the late founder Raymond, who dedicated 25 years of his life to making the little storefront place something special before he passed away more than a decade ago. The restaurant is unpretentious and low key, looking like a throwback to the 1960s or 1970s. The menu is posted on the wall, and the food is what it's all about.

The ribs are huge, delicious, and dripping with sauce. The pork shoulder is perfectly smoked. The specialty of the house seems to be Cornish hen, though—and I truly recommend ordering this if you typically default to chicken in a barbecue restaurant. You can pull them apart as easily as you can chicken cooked to shred, and the flavor is succulent. Even if you would usually order ribs or a pork sandwich, take a chance on this one on your first visit to Cozy Corner.

This is also a place where you want to go out on a limb and check out the barbecue spaghetti—the noodles, cooked to ultimate softness, melt away in your mouth.

As is frequent in African American–owned joints, there's a lot of sauce. Cozy Corner's sauce is a little spicy and very flavorful. Rib tips are on the menu, and so is smoked bologna, which I haven't tried but hear is well worth the order, even in a town that has embraced the concept for a while. For dessert, there's pie and banana pudding as well as sweet Memphis Mudd.

The prices are ridiculously low for what you get, the atmosphere is welcoming, and the whole experience really is worth your drive. Closed Sunday.

Germantown Commissary

2290 Germantown Rd., Germantown, TN 38138; (901) 754-5540; commissarybbq.com

Walker Taylor started Germantown Commissary in 1981 after buying an old country grocery store his father had owned in the Germantown neighborhood (now pretty suburban but still the source of excellent barbecue). Taylor, only a few years out of college, had been waiting tables and doing some catering with his barbecue at the time, and the old commissary offered him a perfect opportunity.

Taylor says they prepare their meats on a combination of charcoal and wood, usually hickory or green oak. "It's getting harder to find hickory, there are only so many trees," he says meditatively. "I'm not so much a purist, I use some green oak; it makes for a fine flavor. My bigger concern is that I source the finest-quality meats I can; I don't rush to cook it; I don't cut corners."

You won't find beef on the menu at the Commissary, but the pork and ribs are pretty terrific. They dry rub the ribs, then finish them with a light baste about half an hour before they come off just to make sure the meat remains juicy. "The shoulders I just put on and let go," says Taylor.

If you want the real dirt on where the famous barbecue nachos come from, it's here. Around 1982, a lady named Rosie Mabon was working for Taylor, and she chanced to add a bit of barbecue to the nacho plate. People saw it and ordered it, and it grew into quite the thing.

These barbecue nachos rock: chips fried on the premises and the best-quality cheese, meat, sauce, and jalapeños. Nothing else to adulterate them: That's that. And if you're in a Southwest frame of mind, grab the paper-wrapped tamales while you're at it.

Everything here is homemade—they'll go through 300 dozen (you read that number right) eggs each week for their deviled eggs. The beer battered onion rings are a thing of beauty next to the pork shoulder sandwich. And save room for pie when all's said and done.

"I hope we meet people's expectations," says Taylor. "If they haven't heard much about us, I hope we exceed any preconceived notions they have." He aims to please. Germantown Commissary does just fine with that.

Gridley's Bar-B-Q

6842 Stage Rd., Bartlett, TN 38134; (901) 377-8055

Gridley's was a chain, once upon a time, with a bit of dominance in the Memphis region, but these days there's just one location left. That single store sits in a strip center in Bartlett, with a front that looks like it still is a chain—but don't let the looks deceive you. Inside you'll find an excellent selection of food with attention to detail by the staff.

This is another of the places Jim Holt raved about to me, and the tender ribs justify the praise he offered up. The pulled pork is darned good too, and most come served with big, beer battered onion rings. The menu is diverse—you'll find the kinds of things that have built Memphis's reputation, including barbecue spaghetti, barbecue nachos, and a smoked sausage and cheese platter. You'll also find tamales and a barbecue burrito, which patrons seem to favor. The smoked ham and smoked sausage plates make good choices as well. Both the hot and the mild sauces please the palate.

There's a lot for potential sides, including the standard potato salad and coleslaw, but fries and onion rings are most popular. You'll find tea, coffee, and soft drinks as beverage options. For dessert, the pecan pie is delicious.

The atmosphere is warm, the staff is friendly, and the decor features lots of old Memphis memorabilia.

Jim Neely's Interstate Barbecue

2265 S. Third St., Memphis, TN 38109, (901) 775-2304; 150 W. Stateline Rd., Southaven, MS 38671, (662) 393-5699; interstatebarbecue.com

Thanks to the Food Network, the Neely name is well known across the country if not the globe—and there's a whole lot to love about *Down Home with the Neely's*. But the now-shuttered Neely's restaurants are the work of Jim Neely's

Something Completely Different

The following dishes are things you see regularly on menus in Memphis and beyond. Take the risk and try them, and you won't regret it for a moment—unless you're watching your waistline.

Barbecue Baked Potato—If you haven't seen this one, you're not trying. Even some of the big chains offer them now; but then, what's not to like? This is pretty mainstream food, but if you've got a good big spud, cooked right, with butter, sour cream, and a heaping helping of barbecue, it's a winner—likely topped with green onion. Some restaurants will load you up with abundant ingredients, but the simple version works just fine.

Barbecue Nachos—For a purist, the barbecue nacho is simply freshly fried tortilla chips, good-quality cheese, jalapeños, barbecue sauce, and pulled pork. But read your menu; there are plenty of other ingredients that may make it onto your plate, just as with traditional nachos (think salsa, guacamole, tomatoes, chili, and so on). Many places make the claim they did it first, but the best candidate for that is Rosie Mabon of the Germantown Commissary, who dreamed them up around 1987. Ernie Mellor of Hog Wild Memphis BBQ was certainly one of the early makers and promoters, and plenty of well-known places followed suit, including Neely's Interstate and Charlie Vergos' Rendezvous.

Barbecue Salad—This one is everywhere these days, and it may not be a strictly Tennessee thing at all, but it's become one of my own favorite dishes. I have to admit, my absolute favorite version is at O'Possums in Murfreesboro, where they toss the pulled pork over spring greens with a high-falutin' champagne vinaigrette. I can't get enough of it—this might make me a snob. A more typical version involves a creamier dressing like a ranch, but I like it lighter. My husband's favorite runs to barbecue over one of Pat Martin's iceberg wedge salads with bleu cheese dressing (a very Middle Tennessee thing, the wedge salad).

(continued)

Barbecue Spaghetti—This is another very Memphis dish, but I highly recommend it. The best versions cook up a barbecue sauce long and slow, with a little pulled pork tossed in, getting something that Eric Vernon of The Bar-B-Q Shop calls "a little sweet, a little oily," then allowing it to saturate the noodles until it has an almost Asian noodle consistency. It's more than just tossing noodles with the sauce; you need to cook the two together a little bit once the noodles have been cooked. Almost certainly it has its origins with Mr. Brady Vincent, original owner of what's now The Bar-B-Q Shop in Memphis back in the early 1970s, but there are outstanding versions done in a number of Memphis restaurants, including Neely's Interstate.

nephews, Pat and Tony (rumor has it that the original Neely's location will be reopened in 2015). It's Interstate that made the family's name first, and it remains one of the stellar barbecue joints in Memphis.

Jim Neely started the restaurant as Interstate Grocery in the late 1970s, a bid to help one of his sons start a business after he left the military. Hoping to make it stand out from the crowd, Jim Neely decided to add a barbecue restaurant, studied the art with friends in the business, and built a custom closed pit. The rest, as they say, is history. By the late 1980s, the grocery store had become a thing of the past, and the restaurant was the business.

Of the many well-known barbecue joints in the city, Interstate stands apart from most of the pack. There's not much on this menu you wouldn't want delivered to your table or served up at a catered party (Interstate does indeed cater). If you want a barbecue salad, they do a fine iceberg version. If you want truly fantastic Memphis-style ribs, order them—served with coleslaw and baked beans as well as bread.

Of note, your pork and brisket sandwiches come sliced or chopped, not pulled, but the flavor is outstanding. Neely's offers its own take on barbecue spaghetti and was one of the earlier purveyors of that trend. Feel good ordering an alternate protein as well—the rib tip sandwich is darned good, and they do bologna and smoked sausage as well as chicken and turkey quite well.

Also on the side, you can get fries and onion rings. The dessert menu is rounded out with pecan pie, sweet potato pie, "sock-it-to-me" cake, or a choice of peach or apple cobbler. Don't look for the bar, but my favorite option here is old-school strawberry, grape, and orange soda as well as the better-known flavors. You gotta love a strawberry soda, especially when most people serve up the same old Coke and Pepsi.

There are family combo packs to go, and the price is very moderate. And as mentioned above, if you have a hankering for Memphis ribs, this is one of the very best places from which to have them sent overnight via Memphis-based FedEx. To have your food shipped overnight by FedEx, call (888) 227-2793.

Marlowe's Restaurant and Ribs

4381 Elvis Presley Blvd., Memphis, TN 38116; (901) 332-4159; marlowes memphis.com

Close by Graceland, with shuttle service to and from the hotels in some brilliant pink limos, Marlowe's is a paean to Elvis and a source of excellent ribs to boot. If Elvis really isn't your thing, I urge you to stretch beyond the kitsch in order to try the fall-off-the-bone ribs. The restaurant has been in the family for decades, founded by Tony Gigliotti in the 1970s and now run by his daughter Missy and her husband Mike.

It was Tony who brought his family's Italian food tradition to the restaurant and maintained it, balanced with the Memphis-style barbecue that the place is known for equally well. Marlowe's is clearly aimed at tourists and the nightlife-loving crowds—the hours are noon to 3 a.m., so if you can't sleep and you need ribs, you know where to go via cerise limo from your lodgings (apparently in the winter, the place opens at 4 p.m.).

It's hard to admit in a barbecue book that you hope someone at the table has some pasta with marinara sauce (a house specialty), but there it is. Take your Italian food–loving friends along. However, it's a good bet that most of the folks will still order the ribs, cooked in the kitchen pit.

The menu is extremely diverse, including steaks, catfish, and plenty of standard dinner favorites. Spaghetti and lasagna are absolute standards: old-school Italian, though Memphis-style barbecue spaghetti appears on the other side of the menu too. There's plenty of barbecue, whether you want your pulled pork on a sandwich, over a salad, or on top of potato chips as an appetizer alternative to the Memphis barbecue nacho.

Marlowe's offers a full bar with a solid beer selection, mixed cocktails, and some wine (they seriously need some good Italian wines and Chianti added to the list, though). Mississippi Mud Cake and a "Crispy Creem" Bananas Foster Sundae round out the dessert options with flair.

Memphis Barbecue Co.

709 Desoto Cove, Horn Lake, MS 38637, (662) 536-3763; 1498 Skibo Rd., Fayetteville, NC 28303, (910) 568-3228; 4764 Ashford Dunwoody Rd., Dunwoody, GA 30338; memphisbbqco.com

Melissa Cookston's husband took her to a barbecue competition before they married, and she found herself hooked. "I loved to cook, and I was into sports, I'm very competitive, it was perfect for me," she says. The pair of them formed a fledgling two-person team and set out to master the barbecue world some 17 years ago. In 2007 they quit their other restaurant work to go on the competition circuit full-time, and in 2011 they opened Memphis Barbecue Co. in Horn Lake, just across the Mississippi border from Memphis. They've since opened a second location in Fayetteville, North Carolina, and one in Dunwoody, Georgia, is on the way as of this writing (due in the fall of 2015). With four wins at Memphis in May out of seven times entering, you can guess she knows how to do it right.

Quality is the word here, and don't expect your pork sandwich to be pulled until you order it. Cookston also has some strong opinions on cooking woods—she prefers fruit woods and sometimes pecan to hickory for delicate white meats like pork and chicken, but she'll toss a little hickory on for the beef brisket. "Women have a more delicate palate," she says. "I think with too much hickory, you taste smoke for a long time, especially if you're smoking your hog for 22 hours; I like fruit woods."

Based on her competition experience, all her rubs are her own creation, made in-house, and the sauce ("It's pretty sultry") uses the rub to produce the main flavor profile: "sweet on the front, then salty, then some heat on the finish."

Back to issues of quality, Cookston sources her meats herself and does her homework to make sure you're getting the best. The wet baby back ribs clearly outsell everything else, but the pork sandwich always has myriad fans.

On the side, try the creamy, sour cream–rich potato salad, something she created for a television competition that made it to the menu when the judges raved. The baked beans and coleslaw are crowd-pleasers as well.

You'll find a full bar at the Fayetteville and Dunwoody locations and beer only in Horn Lake.

"We're giving you the best barbecue we're capable of serving," Cookston says. "This is more than just our work, it's our passion, it's intertwined with who we are as a family, and the culture of who we are. We believe in what we do."

The Original Leonard's Pit Barbecue

5465 Fox Plaza Dr., Memphis, TN 38115; (901) 360-1963; leonards barbecue.com

In 1922, around the time Big Bob Gibson was getting his business off the ground down in Decatur, Alabama, a gent named Leonard Heuberger was setting up a tiny shop in Memphis selling his own pulled pork sandwiches with a signature sweet sauce. The shop's popularity grew by leaps and bounds, and soon there was a good-size drive-in. Back in the day, even the King himself, Elvis, came by for a little barbecue.

In 1962, a guy called Dan Brown, then just 15, came to work part-time after his father passed away. A lifelong lover of barbecue, Dan says one of the few times he ever got spanked by his mom was when, at age 9, he crossed a very busy street to walk to Top's and get himself a sandwich all alone. Dan went away to college in 1966, found himself drafted, and came back to Memphis in 1970—married and ready to attend Memphis State on the GI Bill. Leonard had sold to a local corporation by then, but there was still a part-time job for student Dan.

Fast-forward to 1993, when the dwindling corporation wanted to sell and Dan was there to buy—and keep the original style pork sandwich alive for its many fans. These days, there are no outdoor pits, but the pork shoulders are slow cooked over charcoal and hickory in a brick pit and with a gas-fired, wood-burning smoker.

What makes Leonard's distinctive is the sweet, mustard-based coleslaw on the sandwich, which pairs wonderfully well with the sweet, tomato-based sauce (don't look for heavy vinegar or mayo). They've always called the barbecue sauce just "sweet sauce," so if servers make that reference, don't get confused.

The Chains: Tops Bar-B-Que

Tops (topsbarbq.com) dates back to 1952, with owner J. W. Lawson. The current owner, George Messick, joined in the early 1960s and remains the company owner today. They've spread out across the Memphis area, with a dozen or so locations in Tennessee and several more in Arkansas and northern Mississippi. After 60 years, they've perfected a system of cooking, and it's still as good as it was back then, we hear. The fact that they haven't tried to be all things to all people as a chain and have kept with the barbecue has helped maintain that focus and quality.

Even now, with the franchise spread out around Memphis, Tops has remained committed to cooking the old-fashioned way, over an open pit, using hardwood charcoals and a bit of green hickory to impart flavor to its pork shoulders. It takes a good 10 hours of solid cooking, but it's worth it in terms of flavor. They're cooking shoulders mostly, and the result is frankly excellent.

On the menu is pork, beef brisket, ribs, and burgers if you want them, but I'd aim for the pork sandwich here, though the burgers are tasty. Of course, if you have a burger eater in your crowd, the fact that the meat is fresh ground and cooked to order makes this an order of magnitude better than the average trip to a fast-food joint. Beans, potato salad, and coleslaw come as sides, as do French fries and potato chips. Look for soft drinks, lemonade, and iced tea but not for beer.

Tops has remained a local favorite for six decades for a reason, including loyal local customers. It has grown just big enough to serve everyone, without sacrificing its integrity for multiple locations.

A Few More Memphis Barbecue Places to Try

If you're looking for other venues, here are a few to visit. Of note, when this went to press, the Neely's restaurants had closed down for the most part, but rumor has it they might reopen at a future date at the original location at 670 Jefferson Avenue. If that happens, it's definitely worth the trip.

Bear in mind that there's a joint on every corner in and around the city of Memphis. There's no doubt that there are some excellent places just waiting for you to walk in and eat, even if they haven't gotten the word of mouth that others have in recent years.

Alfred's On Beale, 197 Beale St., Memphis, TN 38103; (901) 525-3711; alfreds onbeale.com
Live music venue. Mostly Memphis-style barbecue, some pasta, steaks. Well more than barbecue and an enjoyable meal.

Double J Smokehouse and Saloon, 124 E. G. E. Patterson Ave., Memphis, TN 38103; (901) 347-2648; doublejsmokehouse.com
Barbecue and standard steakhouse fare, full bar. Interesting option: barbecue egg roll appetizer.

Hog Wild & A Moveable Feast Catering Companies, 1291 Tully St., Memphis, TN 38107; (901) 522-WILD (9453); hogwildbbq.com
Ernie Mellor's catering company is the crowd you call if you have an event—business or family to cater. They don't have a storefront, but if your business has a convention, make arrangements with Hog Wild in advance.

Scooter's Bar-B-Que, (901) 412-3885
Like Nashville's Smoke Et Al, Scooter's is a food truck specializing in barbecue. Friends in the know tell me to order the barbecue bologna, which is mighty fine.

On the side, order homemade onion rings and baked beans in an old-fashioned crockery pot. For dessert, they're famous for the lemon icebox pie, going through something like 60 to 80 pies a week.

Leonard's offers a lunch and dinner buffet as well, so come eat your fill of good food. Ribs, brisket, smoked bologna, and more add to the menu, but it's the pork sandwich you really ought to order.

Payne's Original Bar-B-Que
1762 Lamar Ave., Memphis, TN 38114; (901) 272-1523

Payne's has been a single-family operation since its inception in 1972, the same year Candice Payne, granddaughter of then-owner Emily Payne, was born. Emily founded the restaurant with her son, Candice's dad. Both have since passed away, and these days Candice, her mother Flora, and brother Ronald take care of the operation, but the menu is the same scrumptious simplicity it had back in the day.

"I want people to know we're family owned, and we love our customers and visitors," says Candice. The slogan Flora Payne goes by is that "everything is made with love."

Inside the small building (it seats only about 25 people, set as it is inside a former service station, but to-go is always an option) the number one order is the chopped pork sandwich—yes, chopped, not pulled, and cooked over charcoal, with prominent elements of bark left in for great texture and fine flavor. Payne's fans swear by it, as they do the house-made, distinctive tangy sauce right along with it. Especially at the low price, this is one of the best bargains in the city—yum.

There are a few other proteins—look for a darned good smoked bologna and smoked sausages too, but seriously, the whole town comes in for the chopped pork.

There aren't an abundance of fancy sides. Look for brightly colored, mustard-dominant coleslaw (and expect green cabbage here, not purple—I mean, it's got some serious color) and hearty, meaty baked beans or potato chips if you're in the mood for a little saltiness. If you like a mustard slaw, this is a good one. The only dessert option is Memphis butter cookies (a staple locally, and these are clearly not house-made but still are very good).

Drinks are tea, lemonade, and soft drinks. Payne's can fill large orders, but they don't deliver or cater, so you would best plan to pick them up.

Liquor License

Tennessee aims to be a distillery state, and we have quite a few things for you to try and tours to take if you fancy a tipple. A representative sample of places to go (and drinks to order since many of these are served in barbecue restaurants across the state) might look like this:

Jack Daniel's (jackdaniels.com) in Lynchburg and **George Dickel** (georgedickel.com) in Tullahoma are the big grandpappies of the Tennessee whiskey business. I highly recommend both tours, even if dry counties are involved—they're fun and informative, and you can buy both in your home state at most liquor emporiums. Both are owned by larger corporations these days, but they still produce the real thing when it comes to Tennessee-style whiskey.

I admit to being a big fan of Nashville's growing microdistillery culture. Not only does **Corsair Artisan** (corsairdistillery.com) make good bourbon (in their Bowling Green facility) and some of the most creative whiskey you'll ever try, but in Nashville they produce fantastic spiced rum, a red absinthe, some of the best citrus and juniper-forward gin I've had, and many more besides. They're even producing microbrewed beers now, so rumor has it, with the addition of former Bosco's brewmaster Karen Lassiter.

Then detour over and see what's happening at **Speakeasy Spirits**, where they've recently upped the whiskey production significantly. At their campus on 44th Avenue North, you'll get a chance to visit the home of Whisper Creek Tennessee Sipping Cream, but Jeff and Jenny Pennington have plenty more going on, with the forthcoming production of Pennington's Whiskey, plus they produce spirits for a plethora of other brands. While you're in town, pick up some of their Pennington's Strawberry Rye and pair it with Birmingham, Alabama's, Buffalo Rock ginger ale for the best mule cocktail ever.

Prichard's (prichardsdistillery.com) won me over a long time ago with their rum, and now they've jumped into whiskey, so make the time to visit them in Kelso, down toward the Alabama border. If you're in Nashville, visit their new minidistillery at the Fontanel.

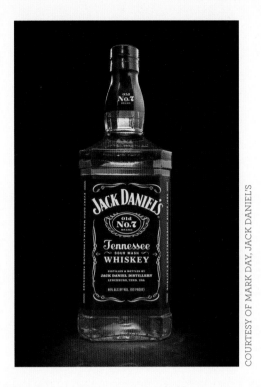

If moonshine strikes your fancy, make the trip to Woodbury to **Short Mountain Distillery** (shortmountaindistillery.com). They also make small batch whiskey and bourbon, and they do it in a scenic and out-of-the-way spot in a beautiful part of the state. This is the best moonshine around, no question.

The brand-new **Tenn South Distillery** (tennsouthdistillery.com) makes some darned good shine too, and don't miss their newly released whiskeys!

A couple of trendy moonshine locales deserve a look-see for tourists: **Ole Smoky** (olesmokey.com) in Gatlinburg and **Popcorn Sutton** in Cocke County (popcornsutton.com) are visitor favorites.

And if you want the story of old-time Tennessee whiskey with a product that makes the best Manhattans around, check out **Nelson's Greenbrier Distillery** (greenbrierdistillery.com) with its new digs in downtown Nashville.

There are 33 small distilleries around the state and also 36 wineries offering a wide variety of varietals across the state—from Memphis to Knoxville and everywhere in between. Drink local while you're here.

Silky O'Sullivan's

183 Beale St., Memphis, TN 38103; (901) 522-9596; silkyosulivans.com

When Jim Holt, CEO of Memphis in May, mentioned Silky's as one of his top 10 favorite places to eat some incredible ribs, there was no question it was going to be in this book. Set in the heart of Beale Street, it's one of those locations you won't have any trouble finding at all. Silky's sits inside the century-old Galina building at the corner of Beale and Third, a credit to the revitalization of the downtown over the past 30 years or more. Of course, as recently as 2007, the Silky's team won best ribs at Memphis in May in the Patio Porkers Division, so that's a sign right there that something good is happening inside.

The atmosphere is upbeat and fun, there's live music, and it's a great place to people watch (especially the patio) and get a sense of the flavor of Beale Street. They have good bar, famed for its hurricanes, and in the evening, if you're lucky, there's the music of dueling pianos (Tuesday through Sunday) and daily live music.

On the wall, there's a collection of signatures from Memphis's music greats and a selection of other stars, from Carl Perkins and Merle Haggard to Bob Hope and Ella Fitzgerald.

On the menu, you can start out with pork or brisket nachos or perhaps some Gulf Oysters if you're up for it. There's a traditional collection of burgers and sandwiches, including pulled pork and brisket, but the ribs are the big deal here, and the servers encourage you to partake of them.

Salads, gumbo, and seasoned fries make up the dominant side items here, and the fudge pie is a nice finish to round out your meal. Take the bar very seriously: The cocktails are plentiful, there's a wine list, and if you're there in the late evening for the music, you can always savor an Irish coffee with your dessert.

Three Little Pigs

5145 Quince Rd., Memphis, TN 38117; (901) 685-7094; threelittlepigs bar-b-q.com

When you can make jokes like "we sell no swine before its time" and get away with it, you'd best serve good food. Three Little Pigs, which has been around since 1989, does just that. The location is yet another small storefront, but don't let the façade scare you away. For one thing, they offer breakfast daily—the kind of epic breakfast that makes you long for the old days—eggs, bacon, ham, sausage, omelets, biscuits, and gravy—even a ham and egg sandwich. Likewise, if you come by in the morning, this is the place to stop.

When it comes to barbecue, there's nothing fancy—it's pulled pork shoulder for the lot of you, pit smoked with hickory and tender, just the way you want it to be. There are, of course, also burgers, fish sandwiches, and grilled cheese, but unless you're 6 years old, pass on those and get yourself pork shoulder. At about $6 for a plate that includes a roll, slaw, beans, and fries, it's a bargain as well.

The sauce is thinner than the usual Memphis option, based, according to the store manager, on a sauce once sold at Loeb's, a local chain that no longer exists but had a plethora of fans.

The side items are fairly simple as well: fries, onion rings, corn, beans, and slaw. The coleslaw and the beans, particularly, win the ribbon for most popular sides. The beans have a bit of pork shoulder in them, and it adds a nice smoky flavor and heartiness to them. The one allowance for barbecue trends here is the availability of barbecue nachos—and they make a nice starter plate if you've got the appetite for one.

The price is very moderate, and the portions are big.

Tom's Bar-B-Q & Deli

4087 New Getwell Rd., Memphis, TN 38118; (901) 365-6690; yelp .com/biz/toms-bar-b-q-and-deli-memphis

Tom's is another of those smaller, almost hole-in-the-wall Memphis locations that blends traditional southern style with Mediterranean spices, proving that the two blend together awfully well yet again. Tom Sturgis, like Charlie Vergos, is a Greek immigrant who works his own culinary heritage into his barbecue. (Having spent a chunk of my early childhood living in Athens, I totally approve.) The current owner is a Palestinian American, Adam Itayem, who continues to underline the close connections between the two styles of cookery with epic success.

It goes without saying that the barbecue on the menu incorporates the usual pork, beef, ribs, and rib tips, plus pit-smoked ham, catfish, and smoked sausage. The rib options are both baby back and beef, and the rib tips are especially inviting. (These had their time on Guy Fieri's show, and they live up to the praise.)

There's also an excellent selection of deli sandwiches on the menu—including chicken salad, tuna salad, and bologna. The sides include things like turnip greens and deviled eggs, which are inevitably popular and surprisingly refreshing on a barbecue joint menu, as well as fries, slaw, potato salad, and beans.

Drink Local: Great Microbrews

Many of the established local barbecue joints maintain local brews on tap. Watch out for the following favorites, all made in Tennessee. If you love barbecue and beer, skip the big names and give the small ones a taste. Most also have tours and tasting rooms—some by appointment only, so if you want to tour, double-check via the websites to make sure of your times.

Calfkiller Brewing Company (calfkillerbeer.com): Named for the Calfkiller River in tiny Sparta, Tennessee, Calfkiller is proof that great brews don't need a big city. Proliferating to more and more restaurants, Calfkiller's Classic Stout, J.Henry Original Mild, and especially the Grassroots Ale deserve trying.

Cool Springs Brewery (coolspringsbrewery.com): Williamson County came slow to the microbrew party, but it's making up for that now. Cool Springs Brewery is producing some terrific craft beers, including the Fatback Amber Ale and the suggestively monickered but wonderful Pecker Wrecker. After that visit, the new Turtle Anarchy (turtleanarchy.com) in Franklin is winning converts too, so make a second trip out for growlers as you go.

Fat Bottom Brewery (fatbottombrewing.com): With its distinctive pinup girl labels, Fat Bottom gets lots of attention, but the East Nashville brewery produces some fine beers. Check out the Black Betty IPA, the Ginger Wheat Ale, or the Bertha Oatmeal Stout.

Ghost River Brewing (ghostriverbrewing.com): Another of the Memphis sources you'll find in many of the area's most well-known barbecue joints, check out the Riverbank Red or Golden Ale, both available all year, or one of the seasonal favorites, like Oktoberfest, Midnight Magic, or Witbier.

Mayday Brewery (maydaybrewery.com): College town Murfreesboro has a high percentage of home brewers, and now they have their own (excellent) brewery. Try the Boro Blonde or the Angry Redhead, and you won't regret your choice.

Saw Works Brewing Company (sawworksbrewing.com): Knoxville's Saw Works has a terrific seasonal Double Chocolate Porter, but year-round, the Brown Ale and Pale Ale make for some good drinking.

Wiseacre Brewing Company (wiseacrebrew.com): Most of the big Memphis barbecue locations offer Wiseacre, either on tap, in cans, or in bottles. Check out the Ananda IPA, Time Bomb, American Pilsner, or one of their specialty beers.

Yazoo (yazoobrew.com): This Nashville-based microbrewery gets national attention lately—and for good reason. Their product is exceptionally drinkable, and they have enough varieties to keep you excited. I'm a big fan of their IPA, but I suspect the real favorite is their Mexican-style Dos Perros, maybe tied with the Bavarian Hefeweizen. You'll find Yazoo constantly in Tennessee, and you can visit at 910 Division Street in Nashville. Down the street, you'll also find Jackalope Brewing (jackalopebrew.com), and that's another good stop, as is Czann's (nashvillebreweries.com/czanns-brewer) over on Lafayette, a few blocks west.

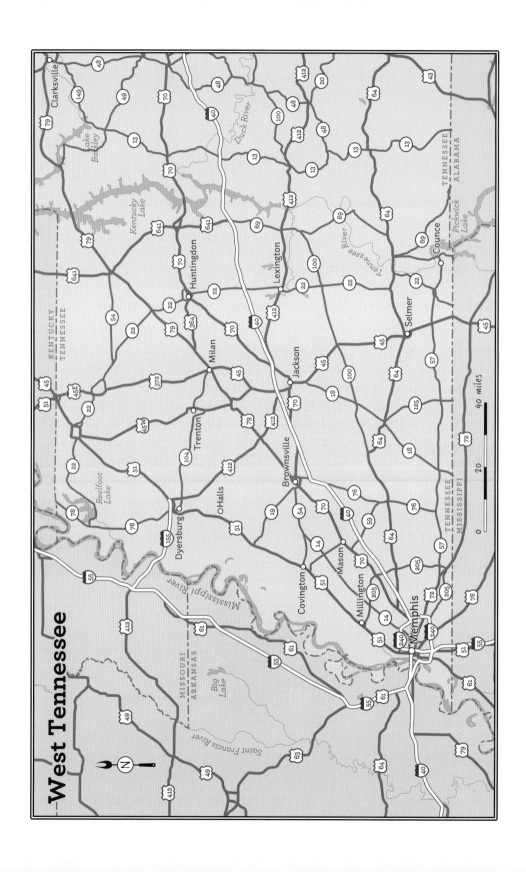

West Tennessee

West Tennessee

West Tennessee probably has more barbecue joints than you can count, although keeping track of them is harder than any other place in the state. Most have no Web page and no details on Yelp or TripAdvisor, and some even have no phone. I've heard high praise for many of them from every person who advised me on this book. Pat Martin learned his barbecue chops here while going to college at Freed-Hardeman. Thomas Williams of Corn bread Consulting is the kind of guy who'll hop in the car or truck on a moment's notice and make a gleeful run along the west-central whole hog belt—or, at least, what used to be the whole hog belt. John T. Edge sings its praises, and he has written an essay or two on it himself.

Yet it's tough to explore when you identify yourself as a journalist. I had three or four restaurants refuse to talk to me while trying to pin this information down—sadly, because they'd all been recently pursued by periodicals that promised them journalistic coverage when what they were really doing is trolling for advertising. That's important to note—first, because I find that kind of pay-for-it journalism sad, and, second, because most of these places have no websites, and some of them have no real phone—best-case scenarios are brief TripAdvisor or Yelp pages and the occasional Facebook page created not by the restaurant but by its regular customers.

But these places, quite simply, do not need all the public relations hustle that joints in larger cities might want. They survive fine all by themselves, with local customers keeping them in business year after year. There's plenty culturally to suggest that the West Tennessee barbecue culture should fade from sight, but instead it's reforming and revising itself. They may not do things exactly the same way it was done 50 or so years ago, but they're making good, good barbecue. It's just different.

Pat Martin sat me down one day and told me about the slow demise of the whole hog barbecue tradition in West Tennessee—something that I've reflected on elsewhere in this book but that bears some repetition for those who skipped the section "A Little History." The short version is that whole hog was once both social occasion and second business for the farmers out here, smoking their hogs overnight on a Thursday or Friday night and selling all weekend until they ran out of meat for sandwiches. It made them extra income.

These days, much has conspired against that world. A few years ago, the USDA plant that supplied the whole hogs burned, Pat says, and after that, not only were hogs scarce, but locals discovered it was infinitely less demanding on both time and expense to start cooking shoulders and butts—so they did. The results are delicious, but the loss of the culture and the skill is fairly tragic for those who remember the old ways with deep nostalgia. One hopes the handful of legacy pitmasters will keep its story going, even if whole hog isn't the common thing any longer.

Added to those concerns, the older generation is no longer so committed, and the children of the old pitmasters are either doing it the new way or not at all.

"Before, you had a family," says Pat Martin. "Dad cooked whole hog, they learned, but grew up and went off to college. The dad is still working 70 hour weeks and cooking barbecue on weekends for extra money Thursday through Saturday, but they reached the point of no real profit. The sons took a 5-day-a-week trucking job or went off to college, aiming for better pay. Rural areas are wealthier than they were, doing better, but it's brought a lot of cultural change. The plant burning was a catalyst for a lot of change. Now, whole hogs are available again, but most of the folks who were doing it have chosen not to go back to the arduous and labor-intensive aspects of barbecue."

Yet there are plenty of places that are inspirational out here. If you limit your stops, my choices are easy. First, Helen's Barbecue in Brownsville, where the dynamic, formidable power house of a female, African American pitmaster Helen Turner, does every single thing on her own, eschewing all the conventions, from seasonings to heavy sauces and extras, and wins everyone's heart doing it. Second, there's Scott's-Parker's, where Zach Parker proves that some pitmasters are willing and able to be heirs to the whole hog tradition and does so with gusto.

But, of course, the best part of West Tennessee is the drive along the back roads around Henderson and Chester Counties. See what turns up; you won't regret it.

Back Yard Bar-Be-Que

186 Old Hickory Blvd., Jackson, TN 38305; (731) 424-7640; backyard bar-be-cue.com

Back Yard Bar-Be-Que is probably best known for their Sunday buffets, country style, which offer their pit-cooked pork shoulder and, for poultry lovers,

West Tennessee Travel

Casey Jones Village: An easy stop off I-40 in Jackson, Casey Jones Village (caseyjones.com) is great for the train lover in every little kid and adult. Among the additional sites here are Providence House—an antebellum event venue, plus the **Casey Jones Home and Railroad Museum,** the Old Country Store, Casey Jones Village Amphitheatre, the Shoppes at Casey Jones Village, Casey Jones Mini-Golf, the Wellwood store with the Wildlife in Wood Studio, and the Judge Milton Brown Pullman Railcar.

Shiloh National Battlefield: As we remember the 150th anniversary of the Civil War, battlefield sites allow us the chance to explore the bloody history of the conflict with teachable moments to learn from. Nearly 110,000 American troops fought in a battle that resulted in 23,746 casualties at Shiloh—more casualties than in all of America's previous wars combined. The beautiful park belies its terrible history (nps.gov/shil/index.htm). Other Civil War sites nearby worth visiting include Parkers Cross Roads Battlefield (parkers crossroads.org) and Johnsonville State Park (tnstateparks.com/parks/about/johnsonville).

Tina Turner Museum: Everyone knows that Tina Turner started out as Anna Mae Bullock in Nutbush, Tennessee, right? Now you can visit the place the gifted rocker studied, the Flagg Grove School, where Tina went for grades 1 through 8. The school was donated to the **West Tennessee Delta Heritage Center** (westtnheritage.com) in 2012 and now serves as a museum honoring her talent. The Heritage Center offers plenty of attractions, including 8,000 square feet of exhibit space, with freshwater aquariums, study of the Hatchie Scenic River, cotton production, and West Tennessee music greats, including Turner.

barbecue chicken and turkey with dressing, all available from 11 a.m. to 2 p.m. for the postchurch and brunch crowd. The atmosphere is warm and welcoming, with checkered tablecloths, wooden tables, and a very country vibe. At about $10 for the buffet per person, it's a great deal.

But if you can't make it in on a Sunday, the restaurant is open daily with a meat-and-three-style menu to inspire your appetite. There's the usual pit-cooked series of specialties, pork (of course), ribs, wings, and beef. You can also get more traditional meat and three lunch counter options, including chicken, delicious burgers, sandwiches, and salads. Ranch dressing dominates the salad options, most of which also include barbecue. If you're a fan of the stuffed barbecue baked potato, this is also a good stop, and don't forget the homemade chili when you order that potato. Barbecue nachos are a house specialty too.

You'll find a host of classic side dishes—the usual suspects plus green beans, corn, or French fries. There are kid's meals—indeed, this is a super-family-friendly restaurant, with an option for just about everyone. Family packs to go can serve up to 16 people.

If you're looking for a place to take the kids, the grandparents, and everyone, Back Yard Bar-Be-Que is designed to suit. (You can call or fax orders to take out as well, with delivery for orders over $12.50.) Jackson has a reputation as a family-friendly town, and this definitely meets those expectations.

Bad Bob's Barbecue

1965 St. John Ave., Dyersburg, TN 38024; (731) 285-4400; badbobs1 .com

Bad Bob's is a smaller chain out of Texas with a solid barbecue menu, including a menu that boasts ribs, barbecue chicken (referred to, as you will here in this state on occasion, as "yardbird" on the menu), Boston butt pulled pork, beef brisket, and smoked sausage for your enjoyment. Let's make note of the use of Boston butt because Big Bob's is proud to showcase this particular cut of pork, and that's a good thing. There is also an assortment of sandwiches, and those extend to barbecue bologna as well as the above-mentioned varieties. Barbecue salads—pork or chicken—can be had as well.

On the side, look for chicken nachos, stuffed baked potatoes, spicy corn, curly fries, breaded pickles, and the usual slaw, beans, and potato salad. Daily specials and takeout are there for the asking, including large family packs. The prices at Bad Bob's are not quite as low as many of the joints in the area but are still on the mild end of the spending zone—and the food is good.

Bozo's Hot Pit Barbecue

342 US 70, Mason, TN 38049; (901) 294-3400; facebook.com/pages/
Bozos-Hot-Pit-Bar-B-Q/182338378461527?fref=ts

Bozo's out in Tipton County, north of Memphis, dates all the way back to 1923 and is named for founder Thomas "Bozo" Williams. (The Southern Foodways Alliance tells the story of an old legal battle over the name with the folks who trademarked a similarly monikered clown.) They've come a long way from those days, but the old-school barbecue still keeps itself at a level that Williams would appreciate. These days, Bozo's sits inside a pleasant brown brick building with green awnings and a genteel façade, offering up a menu full of barbecue options as well as burgers, chicken, catfish, and more. The place has a reputation for good service and friendly staff.

Bozo's meats are served up without sauce. You can add it from the table collection (mild, medium, or hot) if you so desire, but it really isn't necessary. The pulled pork is a star on the menu; I suggest that's your first order. The sides are the usuals, like slaw, mac and cheese, and beans, but they're sizable portions and quite good. There are also plenty of additional main courses, like barbecue bologna, a BLT, grilled cheese sandwich, catfish, and burgers.

On the side, the slaw is sweet and Memphis style, nothing real spicy about it. Mashed potatoes, fries, and onion rings are there, as are Memphis-standards barbecue baked potatoes and barbecue nachos. You can get outliers like a jumbo shrimp plate or a fruit plate, even a ribeye: but really, you're here for the pork (think about the rib plate). Make certain, however, that you order Mrs. Perry's desserts. Her pies are heavenly, and if you skip them, you'll be doing yourself an epic disservice. Closed Monday.

Dave's Smokehouse Grill

93 College Dr., Lexington, TN 38351; (731) 249-5941; facebook.com/DavesSmokehouseGrill

Owner David Williams has spent 40 years in the restaurant business, starting when he was just a kid. With experience ranging from fast food to pizzerias, Williams found himself fascinated by the whole idea of barbecue several years ago. Knowing he wanted a restaurant, he and his wife toured the region, trying barbecue all over, getting ideas and doing research. The result is Dave's Smokehouse. "I knew I wasn't going to do the old-school style, staying up all night over a pit, that's not my thing. So I found the best way to do what felt right to me," he says with confidence, adding that he prioritizes food quality.

Williams uses a pellet smoker of the type frequently utilized by competition barbecue teams, using hickory wood pellets to impart the color and flavor he wants to achieve with his pork butts. The meat gets smoked overnight with a dry rub to create a bark at 225°F. The result is a flavorful, lean pulled pork that customers love.

At Dave's, you'll also find St. Louis–style ribs on the menu (a little meatier than the usual baby back), a beef brisket (Williams toured Austin, researching Texas brisket when he decided to add it to the menu), smoked wings, smoked chicken halves, and bologna. While the pork is most in demand, the ribs are a close second. Look for just two sauces—a sweet, Memphis-style mild and a thinner, more vinegary hot.

Choose from a solid variety of house-made side items, including baked beans, a mayo-based potato salad, coleslaw, and the likes of

baked apples, fried okra, and thick, satisfying onion rings. For dessert, you must try the sour cream coconut cake, made with condensed milk soaked in tres leches style. There are plenty of sweets, but the pecan pie is also exceptional. Save room.

Soft drinks, tea, and lemonade round out the beverage menu, but those wanting beer can bring their own for a $3 convenience fee, which includes a bucket of ice to make sure your six-pack stays frosty.

Catering is available.

Helen's BarBQ

1016 N. Washington Ave., Brownsville, TN 38012; (731) 779-3255

Helen Turner has received a lot of press for her small barbecue joint, all of it deserved. She doesn't serve a whole lot of variety, but what she does she does in an epic way, and you won't leave unsatisfied. Helen is her own pitmaster, and she doesn't have a staff; what she does have are a few relations who come in and lend a hand when she's busy, including her husband, who lights the fires in her barbecue pits, but it's all Helen at the heart of it. And it's delicious.

She, like a handful of other women in this business, is a reminder that barbecue need not be solely the territory of men.

This has been her place for 18 years; prior to that, she worked part-time for the owners. They sold it originally to Mr. Dewitt Foster, who brought her in to help out (though she had previously quit working for his predecessors and moved on). When Foster got ready to retire, he passed the reins on to Helen, and the rest is, as they say, history. Over the next 18 years, she earned a reputation that echoes across the Southern Foodways Alliance to the hallowed halls of *Southern Living* and assorted culinary and southern culture magazines.

When I talk to her, she has 12 whole shoulders smoking over her hickory and oak fires. "I don't use charcoal," she says. "I didn't even learn how to use charcoal until I went to a food and wine festival in San Francisco, and they'd brought out a bunch of different barbecue people, cooking different ways."

When you order, be aware that Helen doesn't dry rub, wet mop, marinate, or inject her meat—there's no seasoning, just slow smoking. If you want sauce, she'll give it to you, but it's all about the flavor of the meat. In addition to pork shoulder, look for ribs and barbecue bologna.

Sides are straightforward—baked beans, coleslaw (Helen is inclined to put it on your sandwich, but on the side is an option), and potato salad. Soft drinks (no beer to drink), and don't worry about dessert—you'll be too full.

"Most of the time, being here feels like you're at home," she says. "There are no strangers to me. Sit down and tell me what you want." Closed Sunday.

I-40 Exit 87 Barbecue Stand

2049 US 70 E., Jackson, TN 38305; (731) 988-6222; facebook.com/pages/I-40-Exit-87-BBQ-Stand/175077839189772

Reviving the old-school tradition of the roadside stand right off the interstate, this is a great easy stop on your drive west. This is old-fashioned hickory smoked pulled pork at a bargain price, open at 7 a.m. and closing whenever they sell out of pork. You have to love that in a barbecue joint, right? The Barbecue Stand is a tribute to the way things used to be, updated for a contemporary audience with nothing sacrificed to trends. Happily, they now take debit and credit cards instead of just cash.

The early opening means barbecue sandwiches for breakfast, and plenty of people head over here as opposed to the generic truck stop across the road. The hours mean you'll find a mix of locals, tourists, truckers, and travelers mixing together at the tiny mobile stand that owners Josh and Judy Wadley have operated for about 5 years now.

The menu itself isn't huge—pulled pork, St. Louis–style ribs, barbecue chicken quarters, hot dogs and chili dogs, barbecue nachos, and bologna. The unique choice is the potato dog—a hefty hot dog stuffed with potato salad (seriously, try it). Soft drinks are the only beverages to be had. Take out or eat in front of the stand on picnic tables, rain or shine. You can get family packs and the like to go.

Note that the hours really are sporadic in terms of when they close. When they run out of the day's barbecue, they're done until tomorrow.

Joe's Diner Family-Style Restaurant (Joe's Bar-B-Que)

19190 W. Main St., Huntingdon, TN 38344; (731) 535-3377

Also known to locals as Joe's Bar-B-Que, Joe's is a cafeteria-style restaurant of the type once prevalent across the region, now sadly going even faster than the hole-in-the-wall barbecue joint. What's important here is that they also cook some serious barbecue ribs, slow cooked to perfection over charcoal, and some pretty serious barbecue chicken as well, among other options.

While we're at it, there are hot wings, pork and beef barbecue, and plenty more. There's a meat-and-three style to the menu (think an even more rustic version of Arnold's in Nashville), where lunch offers up a few different meat options, changing daily, and an assortment of sides to choose from. Beyond the barbecue, look for meatloaf, hog jowl, and Salisbury steak. Because they have such a broad menu, the catering options are extensive as well.

Joe's is the kind of "little bit of everything" place my grandparents used to love, and there's a warm, family-centric atmosphere. The desserts are plentiful, rich, and delicious—make sure you save room for the day's cake or cobbler. Don't expect a bar, froufrou decor, or any kind of chain restaurant–inspired fern bar decoration, just the kind of really old-school southern cooking that helped give us the culinary reputation in the first place.

Little Porky's Pit Barbecue

105 Mueller Brass Rd., Covington, TN 38019; (901) 476-7165; little porkysbbq.com

Set in Covington, Little Porky's is one of those just-outside Memphis-area stops in Tipton County you should make. The restaurant has been operated by the Uttz family for nearly 50 years now, having had more than one location over time—thanks to natural disaster and more. They take their barbecue seriously (and also the catfish, lest you have a question about that). The current incarnation is set in a brick strip center, with a wonderfully kitschy interior, full of old-time advertising signs, pig decor, brick, and barn wood (not to mention the odd pool table).

The menu is heavy in the Memphis-area favorites, ranging from starters like barbecue nachos and hot wings to entrees of pork shoulder, ribs, shredded beef brisket, and barbecue chicken. The ribs get plenty of compliments, as does the catfish, which is a long-term menu staple and typical at barbecue restaurants in the area (where it's usually fried, not smoked). Burgers and sandwiches round out the menu.

Side items include the staples, plus mac and cheese, green beans, mashed potatoes and gravy, and spicy fries. You can also get a catfish filet on the side with your barbecue, thus mixing the best of both worlds. Soft drinks are served (no alcohol). There's a kid-friendly menu as well, including grilled cheese and chicken strips as well as barbecue. For dessert, try a fried pie or soft-serve ice cream as well as banana pudding. Catering and takeout are available for large and small groups.

Mackenzie's BBQ

2857 SR 70 W., Jackson, TN 38301; (731) 424-9650; mackenziesbbq.com

This combined grocery stop and barbecue restaurant has a little bit of everything. The original restaurant was founded in 1918 by John Mackenzie, and while the place is considerably more contemporary in appearance and vibe today, the barbecue remains good. In a region that loves its barbecue traditions, having that old name is a good thing. On the weekends, there's a barbecue buffet, but the off-the-menu options during the week make for excellent dining.

Breakfast is made up of good old country favorites—bacon, chicken, or ham biscuits; sausage, egg, and cheese on toast; ham and eggs; and so on. Lunch offers up hickory-smoked pulled pork sandwiches, as well as more traditional meat and three, with the slaw, beans, and potato salad that pair with the barbecue as the most popular side items. Hamburgers are big on this menu, especially for dinner, and you'll also find cheesesteaks, gyros, and fish and chicken sandwiches.

The dining room has the kind of fun southern and/or western wooden kitsch that chain restaurants copy with far less success (check out the fighter plane hanging over your head and the big wooden rockers for relaxing). It's a good place to bring the family. Of course, there's a full market as well, so you can pick up groceries and grab barbecue to go at the same time.

Neil's Barbecue and Grill

470 Mall Blvd., Dyersburg, TN 38024; (731) 285-2628; facebook.com/neilsbbqtn

Neil's has been a staple in the area since the late 1980s, with a menu that stretches well beyond just barbecue. Be prepared for the fact that it's located in a strip center, but the food is high quality and the menu diverse—and the interior is far more charming. They have a reputation for good service. It's a restaurant of the sit-down variety, not a true joint, and expect the bill to reflect that.

The appetizers include things like potato skins, fried cheese, and sautéed mushrooms, perhaps geared more to the folks who aim for the chains in terms of selections. When you get to sandwiches and entrees, you'll feel more of a sense of a barbecue place—pulled pork, brisket, smoked sausage, barbecue bologna, and smoked turkey all have prime places. Barbecue salads and loaded baked potatoes are also there. Dinner options expand to a big rib plate, chicken dinner, and country fried steak—and even bigger to prime rib and filet at market price.

Side dishes offer up a vinegar slaw, barbecue beans, potato salad, fries, onion rings, and the above-mentioned sautéed mushrooms. You can grab a beer with your barbecue here, as well as a soft drink, and though the beer menu is limited, they still go down cold.

Neil's is more the nicer meal out with family than the kind of place you just sit down with your buds for a sandwich, but there's nothing bad about that.

Old Timers Restaurant

7918 C St., Millington, TN 38053; (901) 872-6464; oldtimers restaurant.com

Old Timers marks its start as 1985, but the building has been around rather longer when it comes down to it. When you walk in, you find yourself surrounded by a massive collection of old pictures, dating back to the early part of the 20th century and chronicling building and area history, including its railroad history. The place itself was built as a hardware store here before World War I. It's a fascinating place to visit: full of curiosities. Old Timers is not limited to barbecue—they have a rather extensive menu stretching all over the place, with specials daily.

Rest assured, however, that there's a barbecue pit and plenty of options coming out of the smoke there. You can get your barbecue pork sandwich, a rack of ribs served wet or dry, and smoked chicken quarters with ease. You can also order a pit-smoked chicken salad if you're fond of a barbecue salad option.

This is the kind of place that also offers a real abundance of side items, so you can have the usual or branch out a bit for turnip greens, field peas, or mashed potatoes with ease. There's a kid's menu that provides a barbecue pork sandwich as well. Daily specials tend toward Cajun or Italian offerings, along with southern-style comfort food.

There's an abundant breakfast menu as well, which, while not full of barbecue, make this a great stop if you happen to be touring through the area. Finally, there's also a bar, with mixed drinks, an assortment of domestic beer, and a few wine options that pair appropriately with the dinner menu. Takeout is available for all menu items, but calling in advance to order is highly recommended.

Pappy John's Original Barbecue

SR 45 S., Selmer, TN 38375; (731) 645-4353

Pappy John's is a real old-school barbecue joint. Kenneth Locke, then in the lumber business, and his wife, Louise, bought the place in 1984 and hired a pitmaster to run it for them. When he passed away several years later, they took over. Neither of them came from a barbecue family, but they learned and have made a very successful go of it.

Louise says most of their advertising comes by word of mouth. "We had a gentleman in here not long ago, he was a trucker, and he said, 'You'll never guess where I heard about how good you all were—in Arizona!'" Likewise, don't look for a formal website or any details—the place is open 9 a.m. to 7 p.m. weekdays, until 8 p.m. on Friday and Saturday, and 10 a.m. to 4 p.m. on Sunday.

They use a wet mop method of cooking, with an electric cooker liberally dosed with hickory wood chips to infuse the rich, smoky flavor of the wood. Keeping with the current market, their pork is shoulders and hams. Also on the menu are ribs, chicken (you can get half or order a whole), and barbecue bologna. "That's really popular with the men," says Louise. "The women tend to favor chicken and sometimes pork."

Overall, though, it's pork and ribs that are bestsellers. The side items are few—baked beans, slaw, and potato salad—but they fill the plate nicely. Soft drinks and tea are readily available, and if you want dessert, there are bakery cookies. You'll fill up on the meal itself.

"The first thing we tell people is just how good it is," says Louise. "If you give them a little taste, they'll start to order right away. Stop on by, the food's delicious."

While Pappy John's doesn't cater per se, they'll deliver food for your group if you order it.

Paul Latham's Meat Company and Barbecue
3517 US Hwy. 45 N., Jackson, TN 38305; (731) 664-0073

Latham's is one of those things you find in the South on occasion, a combination restaurant and butcher shop. They used to be a little more common than they are now, but rest assured, you want to make this stop and try the tender juicy pulled pork they're making. They offer up whole hog barbecue (yes, blessedly real whole hog), and visitors praise the dry-cooked ribs (you'll find sauce on the table, both mild and hot if you wish it). The actual cooking takes place out back behind the butcher's shop and restaurant in a little cinder-block outbuilding, where the meat is prepared over hickory charcoal.

It's almost easy to pass this restaurant by, given that it's clearly a butcher shop, but don't. Go in and have a sandwich, some barbecue bologna or ribs, your vegetable choices (sides and desserts vary daily, but expect a good variety), and a soft drink, then, if it strikes your fancy and you have a cooler, wander into the butcher shop part of the equation and pick up that slab of bacon or ham you need to take home.

There are breakfast (6 a.m. to noon) and lunch (noon to 2 p.m.) buffets offered for the ridiculous sum of $5.99 that will keep you filled up for the whole day—no wonder Latham's is so popular with local residents. While the food here is unquestionably good, it's the whole environment that makes this one— market on one side, restaurant on the other. If you're looking for something that underlines the old West Tennessee culture, stop in and order a meal.

Be warned, these are big portions. And for those who crave dessert, the old-fashioned fried pies truly taste incredible.

The meat market, by the way, will cut meat to order; you have more than just supermarket-style packages to opt from—they also grind their hamburger themselves and even make a selection of fresh sausages. If you have a taste for pork rinds, pick up a package of fresh cracklings. To-go and catering available.

Pig House BBQ

1024 Campbell St., Jackson, TN 38301; pighousebbq.com

Pig House is set in a cinder-block building behind a local chain drugstore, and don't expect to come marching in for a sit-down meal. This place is and has always been a drive-through restaurant, but the owners, Dave and Keith Clifton, are in regularly and make a practice of being part of your drive-through experience. That makes for good customer service, and fortunately the food is worth driving to pick up. And with more than 25 years of history behind it (they opened in 1987), they've kept customers coming. The family has been in the restaurant business for something close to a century, and it shows in the amount of care they put into the menu. If you need to take home a lot—or you need to cater an event—they can manage that too.

Like most barbecue joints in the area, the menu is dominated by pulled pork, with the requisite hickory smoke. If you're looking for lunch, a regular barbecue sandwich with chips and a drink comes in at about $6. Weekends only, you can also get barbecue chicken, either with sides or a bun, or a whole or half chicken to go. For around $20, you can take home a pound and a half of pork with sauce, slaw, baked beans, and chips to feed the family.

If you want to try it long distance, orders can be placed by calling the restaurant. You can also place holiday orders to serve up for Thanksgiving and Christmas. Closed Sunday.

Pig-N-Out

225 N. Front St., Halls, TN 38040; (731) 836-5353; facebook.com/pignout1995

Pig-N-Out is definitely a joint—nothing at all fancy—with a menu over the counter where you order, red checkered tablecloths, and wood chairs—the kind of place you picture when you imagine eating Tennessee barbecue. The prices are cheap, the atmosphere's legit, and it's a fun place to come on in for a meal.

The current menu starts out with barbecue pork sandwiches, then moves on to offer you barbecue bologna, smoked turkey, hot ham and cheese, a good burger or cheeseburger, or loaded baked potatoes with pork or grilled chicken and grilled shrimp. On the side, look for fries, tater tots, onions rings, slaw, beans, or potato salad. If you want ribs, it best be a Friday or Saturday night, but it's worth waiting for the right day to get them. Hot wings and barbecue nachos are there to start you off.

To drink, it's soft drinks only. Family to-go packs start at $19.99.

Pig-N-Out is a casual, friendly, bring-your-kids-in kind of place that you'll be glad you stopped by for.

R&B Barbecue and Restaurant

7285 Tennessee 57, Counce, TN 38326; (731) 689-1999

The exterior of R&B (that's Robbie and Beau) may look unprepossessing, but once you get inside and try the food, you won't care. Set in a refurbished old garage, R&B takes their cuisine far more seriously than their outside might suggest. Their slogan is "Been Smokin' since 1979"—incidentally the year Beau was born as dad Robbie Meter was learning the ins and outs of barbecue at Mayhall's (as this place was called before the Meters bought it). The father-and-son team smoke their meats in a pit using hickory wood—pork shoulders, ribs (dry rub), chickens (wet mop), sausages, bologna, and, at holiday time, some of the best turkeys you've ever had.

"I know people like their fried turkeys," says Beau Meter, but the way we smoke them really locks the moisture in, makes them juicy—it's so good." If you're headed through West Tennessee in November, it might be wise to order one. You might even make the drive specially.

The little place seats about 89 people. They open early for breakfast, so you can start your day with an omelet and go from there. The pulled pork and ribs are top sellers, but there are some weekend specials to be aware of. Friday night dinners mean whole smoked chickens—so popular that they're often sold out before Beau's finished cooking them. On Saturday night, it's all about ribs and Beau's smoked ribeye steaks.

There are plenty of sides to select from, but the home fries and onion rings win customer-favorite bragging rights. For dessert, consider the house-made chocolate and coconut cake, plus pecan or apple pie.

Luckily, there's beer by the can and bottle, so you can wash down your barbecue with a cold one. Across the board, you're not likely to leave with any appetite remaining after a meal at R&B.

Other West Tennessee Locations

As I've said, this is an area you can stop anywhere you want to and get some good barbecue. Here are a few more places worth your while. Some of them still manage some whole hog, though few are doing it as the entirety of the menu any longer. If you really want whole hog, Liz's is probably the best bet beyond Scott's-Parker's. But any of these locations have more than enough real barbecue credit, and all of them deserve your attention.

While you're at it, if you can make the small but friendly Chester County Barbecue Festival, it's a direct contrast to the bigger shows like Jack Daniel's and Memphis in May—a true rural festival where all the pride is in the cooking.

Bill's Latham's Barbecue, 535 S. Church Ave., Henderson, TN 38340; (731) 989-4075
One of the last of the whole hog guys, Bill Latham has switched over to ribs and shoulders since health concerns prevented him from lifting a pig like he used to—but you can rely on this place for good old-fashioned pulled pork sandwiches that give you something to smile about. Real good barbecue, that's all that matters.

Liz's Bar-B-Q, 311 S. Church Ave., Henderson, TN 38340; (731) 983-0400
This is one of the "don't judge a book by its cover" locations—it's quaint but definitely not competing for most-beautiful-restaurant status. But forget appearances. Liz's is still cooking whole hog, and the pulled pork you get here is nothing short of phenomenal. The meat is smoked over hickory wood, and the smoky flavor is just perfect. If you want to taste real whole hog, you don't have too many options. This is a fine one.

Mac's BBQ, 630 Hollywood Dr., Jackson, TN 38301; (731) 265-9771
They don't much have time for the phone if you call, but both the food and the service here are exceptional, so I'm willing to forgive that one. Mac is clearly a lovely man, from my brief words with him. The pulled pork is everything you'd want it to be and more, the brisket is terrific, and Mac's deserves your time.

(continued)

Papa KayJoe's, 119 W. Ward St., Centerville, TN 37033; (931) 729-2131
This is one of those completely unprepossessing locations, set in a great little brown building that looks like a million bait and tackle shops you've passed, but inside it's full of fantastic things. You'll find pulled pork served up on a hoecake (corn bread pancake), and it's completely wonderful—quite the contrast to a soft white bon and so delicious.

Richard's Bar-B-Q, 413 W. Jackson St., Bolivar, TN 38008; (731) 658-7652
For more than 20 years, Richard and Debra Hodge have produced monstrously good barbecue at this Bolivar location. They cook up some excellent pork shoulder you really don't want to miss, once again in a tiny little place that doesn't look like much from the road. If you learn nothing else from this book, remember that what a place looks like on the outside has nothing to do with the quality of the barbecue—otherwise, you might miss true gems like this one.

Siler's Old Time BBQ, 6060 SR 100, Henderson, TN 38340; (731) 989-2242
Siler's is one of the Henderson, Tennessee, legends that people tend to wax truly poetic about. The whole hog tradition is still going out here, and Chris Siler, who has owned the place for the past 6 or 7 years, also cooks butts—taught by previous owner Ronnie Hampton. Popular rumor has it that there's been a pit cooking hog on this spot since the Civil War and maybe before. While there's no website, you can find plenty of information on the owner and the restaurant's history at the Southern Foodways Alliance (southernfoodways.org).

Reggi's Hickory Pit Barbecue and Wings

292 Parkstone Place, Jackson, TN 38305; (731) 660-8600; reggisbbq
.com

Reggi's is set in a pretty little strip center that implies it might be a bit more
fancy than it is, what with the high beam ceilings, concrete floors, and exposed
brick exterior—but trust me, it's super homey when you get inside, and this is
good, down-home, slow-cooked barbecue. It's a family-run restaurant, with far
more than just barbecue, though the specialty of the house is undoubtedly the
barbecue.

When you start out here, go for the wings. There's a great list of original
recipe sauces, and if you like them, you can buy a bottle and take it home.
Heck, make a meal of the wings, they're worth it. (Warning: Try the Suicide and
Inferno sauces at your own risk.)

Sandwiches are abundant, and Reggi's offers more than the expected.
With Memphis style in mind, you'll find barbecue bologna, polish sausage,
and rib tips. On the specialty menu, take a gander at the Monterey Chicken
Sandwich. The side options go from the usual slaw, baked beans, and potato
salad to fries, onion rings, and fried okra (we in the South really like our corn-
meal battered fried okra, and we understand that it isn't typical elsewhere; I
always pick the okra).

There is a drive-through window for those wishing to grab and go, delivery can be arranged, and catering is definitely available across the West
Tennessee region. You can also order the famous sauces by calling the restaurant, even if you need them shipped halfway across the world. Closed
Sunday.

Scott's-Parker's Barbecue

10880 US 412 W., Lexington, TN 38351; (731) 968-0420; facebook
.com/scottsparkersbarbeque

For a variety of reasons, ranging from economics to changing times and skill
sets among barbecue pitmasters, there's not a lot of dedicated whole hog barbecue culture out there anymore. That's a shame because once upon a time,
this part of West Tennessee was all about whole hog. But Zack Parker still carries on the tradition—one he learned from his father, Ricky Parker, which he in
turn learned from the store's original owner, Early Scott. Ricky Parker himself
was a legend in the world of Tennessee barbecue. He passed away in 2013,
leaving Scott's-Parker's to his sons; these days, Zack is the guy running it and
cooking whole hog. It's one of the last bastions of the art, no question.

Parker sources his wood, all hickory, that quintessential element of Tennessee barbecue, from a sawmill in Savannah Tennessee. With it, he pit smokes his hogs for 18 to 24 hours. "You have to know exactly what you're doing," he says. "I don't use a thermometer like some places. I've got the hogs covered up, smoking up to 22 at a time if need be. You've got to stay out there, watch for grease fires that flare up and other problems. The work is long hours, real stressful—but it's the way I was raised up, the only way in my mind, to do it." In a word, it's dedication.

Whole hog is a very different taste than the usual smoked lean butts and shoulders. It doesn't dry out if cooked properly, and you can expect a fair amount of fat—it's rich, juicy meat that falls apart in your mouth.

In addition to pulled pork, Parker will offer up things like chicken and smoked bologna, and he also does specialty parties. Ask, and he'll tell you about smoking quail for local lawyers and judges who have brought an abundance back from a hunt and bring in 30 to 50 people for a special party. (If it takes skill to cook whole hog, it takes plenty to properly cook tiny game birds as well.)

Go in and order a pork sandwich. Add some slaw, baked beans, or a pork sandwich. For dessert, there are fried pies—apple, peach or chocolate. Don't forget to order a barbecue baked potato because these are a fine thing—absolutely fantastic.

If you're making a drive across Tennessee looking for places to stop, this is a must-visit.

Smokin' Hot Barbecue Drive In

13005 S. First St., Milan, TN 38358; (731) 487-7790; smokinhotbbq .webs.com

Smokin' Hot is indeed a drive-through, and expect the lines around lunch or dinner time to be long at the unprepossessing red-painted building in Milan. Everything is made on-site, and it's not a fancy menu filled with extras, just good barbecue and traditional side items. Even the soft drinks—cans only— are pretty low maintenance. In addition to the regular menu, look for specials that set Smokin' Hot apart from the crowd, like their dipped cheeseburger— smothered in molten cheese to the point of insanity (made for the cheese lover, trust me).

On the daily menu, look for barbecue pork, brisket, chicken, turkey, smoked bologna, and ribs, all ready to go—whether by plate, sandwich, or family meal pack. Meats can also simply be purchased by the pound.

When it comes to side, they too are straightforward—beans, potato salad, chips, or a choice of either mayo or vinegar slaw, all made on the premises. Barbecue salads, nachos, and loaded potatoes are there, as is a Memphis-style sausage and cheese plate.

It's all good old-fashioned Memphis style—don't let the name fool you into looking for Texas-esque cheerleader waitresses in tank tops. And do try that dipped cheeseburger, for heaven sakes.

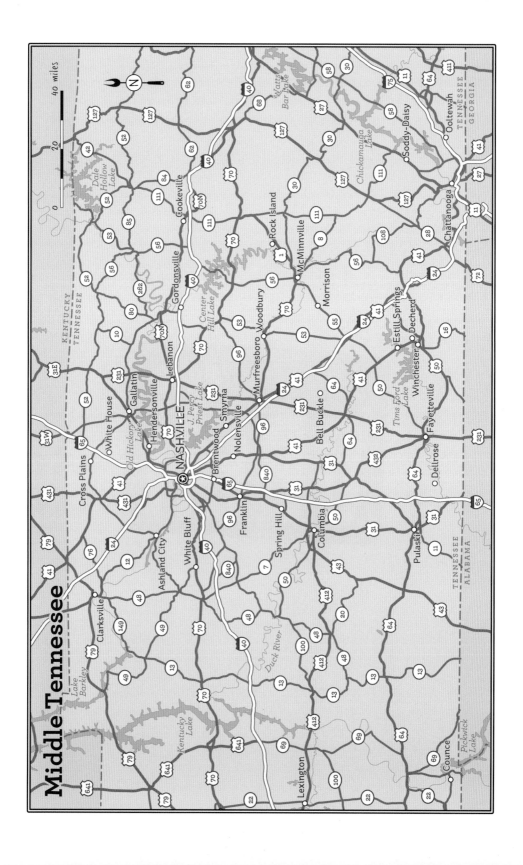

Middle Tennessee

Middle Tennessee

Middle Tennessee isn't really a latecomer to the barbecue field, it just feels like it. Stretching along the I-65 corridor, spreading out east to west along I-24 and I-40, this part of the state has taken the highlights of the region and merged the things it loves most into its best-loved barbecue—but that doesn't mean we didn't have our own ideas too. But as the national media is singing our praises, we have to admit that of many of our most renowned pit-masters come from very specific traditions, from Memphis, West Tennessee, and even Birmingham. And that's not a bad thing—we take the exceptional from those regional traditions, and we run with them.

Middle Tennessee's food community seems to be in a constant state of flux at the moment, and that's not a bad thing. We're growing at a stunning rate of speed, with more options appearing almost daily. By the time this book is published, there will be half a dozen barbecue places that hadn't even been imagined while the book was being written (indeed, Edley's opened their second location during the copy editing).

While the national media appears to focus on a handful of higher-end, nonbarbecue restaurants and the midrange and higher-end genres get an abundance of local publicity as well, barbecue is finally starting to come into its own in the area. In part that's due to pitmasters who have taken their shows to the big time—gaining visibility via the Food Network and HGTV and attendance at major festivals, like Charleston Food and Wine, Atlanta Food and Wine, Big Apple Barbecue, and Memphis in May—and whose dominant personalities stand out from abundant print media attention.

Don't get me wrong. We're proud that we can claim the likes of Peg Leg Porker's Carey Bringle and Patrick Martin of Martin's, that we draw Brett and Catharine Newman of Edley's, and that Molly James decided to use her training with Nick Pihakis of Jim N' Nick's here instead of somewhere else. We have incredible prominent chefs. And we also still get to claim the wonderful off-the-beaten-path stuff, like Carl's Perfect Pig in White Bluff (which is an absolute must-stop).

Not so long ago, just about everything here in the Nashville area was in fact a chain. Not that it was all bad, as there are chains producing pretty reasonable meals out there, but a decade ago, the plethora of Corky's and Whitt's sometimes hid the non-franchise options. That's no longer the case.

Middle Tennessee has always had the same kind of collection of odd barbecue joints that appear along the road, with pitmasters worrying less about financing television commercials and more about smoking pork right. Once you leave the bounds of Nashville, Franklin, Murfreesboro, and such, you'll discover all those little places just off the highway that no one but the locals have ever heard of but that encourage plenty of nonlocals to stop.

Our cooking traditions are all about hickory wood and a sauce that sometimes meets in the middle of the Memphis sweet, tangy style and the slightly vinegar tastes of East Tennessee with its North Carolina influence.

I frequently spend weekends with my husband down at my parent's second home in Rock Island Tennessee (totally not barbecue, but if you're ever there, for the love of God, visit the Foglight Foodhouse in Walling). There are a couple of potential routes from our Franklin home. One involves taking I-40 straight across, where you mostly have standard interstate fast-food chains (except when you get off on Highway 111 in Cookville).

If you need to eat on the way, take I-24 toward Chattanooga and stop off at the Bell Buckle Café. Or, when you get off I-24 at SR 55, you pass myriad tiny places with smokers outside as you travel toward McMinnville (Prater's has an outlet here on SR 55, at 9576 Manchester Highway in Morrison; stop in). A third option is to take the back roads all the way, traveling US 70 south through Murfreesboro (wings from Slick Pig!) through Woodbury and down to McMinnville, again with the tiny joints just waiting for you to discover. Once I'm there, it's pretty much regular trips to the Rock Island Market, one of those tiny holes in the wall. The pulled pork is very good there, but the real secret is the best pie ever in the whole world.

And that's how you should eat down here, not by relying on the fast-food megaplexes but by pulling off at the little places that beckon, with names you've never heard and "Bar-B-Q" on the sign.

B&C Market

(Bacon & Caviar); 900 Rosa L. Parks Blvd. (inside the Nashville Farmers' Market), Nashville, TN, (615) 770-0032; B&C Melrose, 2617 Franklin Pike, Nashville, TN, (615) 457-3473; B&C Ashland City Smokehouse, 1203 Old Hydes Ferry Pike, Ashland City, TN, (615) 792-8889; baconandcaviar.com

I got hooked on B&C when I was working downtown and trying desperately to vary my lunch menu. The Downtown Farmers' Market offers a market house full of outstanding restaurants, and B&C sits right inside the door leading in from the southern market shed. Everything on the menu is specific to the day of the week—but there's always plenty, and protein and two sides is more than enough to have some left over to take home when your husband is off at Muay Thai and you don't want to cook for yourself. I generally favored the smoked chicken breast with sides of cucumbers and tomatoes in a vinaigrette dressing and maybe some green beans, but the roast potatoes sometimes won me over. The smoked salmon, when it's on the menu, is typically delicious.

I have to admit that as good as the proteins are, the sides at B&C are a driving force to help get me in the door. That's far from true at every barbecue joint you visit, but especially at the Downtown Farmers' Market location, you see a lot of folks leaving with containers containing multiple side items—and there's nothing shameful about that.

If you're a dessert lover, the pies, cobblers, and cakes are always a temptation. And if you really, truly need fried food, they will fry to order not only French-fried potatoes but onion rings, chicken wings, and delicious fried pickles as well. (I am fairly sure fried pickles started out as a Texas thing, but Tennessee has appropriated them with aplomb.)

B&C also caters, and you can order proteins by the pound. It's an excellent choice for a catered event.

The Bar-B-Que Place

138 Cliff Garrett Dr., White House, TN 37118; (615) 672-3444; bbq whitehouse.com

White House isn't that hard to reach off I-40 or SR 840, though it's a little off the beaten path. If you're in the area, take the time to drive by the cute little red brick restaurant and grab a bite. The Bar-B-Que Place opened in 2006, and it's still going strong. The restaurant seats just 30—there's a lot of takeout business, and they cater large parties as well.

"Everything here is homemade and cooked to order," says manager Cameron Berry. That's one the things that makes it special. The menu overwhelms with options, and the ribs are easily the most popular item, but consider starting your meal with the barbecue fries or BBQ nachos. Also high on the popularity scale is the array of loaded baked potatoes—ridiculously huge and filling. Topped with butter, sour cream, cheese, and your choice of meat, these are easily a full meal in themselves. Not just barbecue is an option; you can top it with steak if you so desire.

Like most Middle Tennessee locales, they offer you a choice of bun or corn bread—opt for corn bread with your pork barbecue—or the brisket, for that matter.

Desserts live up to the overwhelming level of the baked potato piled with barbecue—the Chess Pie gets raves, but Berry says the Piggy Pudding wins hands down—layers of graham crackers, pudding, cream cheese, and Cool Whip. Wow. Bring an appetite to the Bar-B-Que Place and expect big portions.

Beer in bottles is available in limited variety (Bud Light, etc.)—they're better known for soft drinks and sweet tea.

BB's Bar-B-Q

228 New Hwy. 96 W., Franklin, TN 37064; (615) 599-2750

BB's is one of those little holes in the wall just off SR 96 toward the Natchez Trace, a nice alternative to the many chain fast-food joints that seem to congregate in Williamson County. It's a glorified shack, indeed, but the food coming out is very good. BB's is one of those places that's been there for a while and changed names over the years, so you may remember it as something different.

Drive up, order at the window, and take home your barbecue. Family packs are really what it's all about, though sandwiches are readily available—beef brisket, chicken, turkey, or pork, all smoked and nicely flavored and the usual collection of solid side items. You'll also find smoked wings, ribs that are super tender, and sides that make meals, like Brunswick stew. The corn bread is good.

This is the kind of barbecue joint some people go searching for—the mythical shack full of smoky flavor that writers discuss but that, especially in Middle Tennessee, is becoming less common as larger restaurants take over. I'm glad there are still a few around.

Bell Buckle Café

16 Louisville and Nashville Railroad, Bell Buckle, TN 37020; (931) 389-9693; bellbucklecafe.com

Bell Buckle is a tiny town along I-24 between Nashville and Chattanooga best known for the private, classical Webb School and the Moon Pie Festival held there each spring. It's a delightful discovery, full of antique and trinket shops and myriad 19th- and early 20th-century houses off the school grounds. And there are plenty of folks who plan their drives between the two big cities to time a lunch stop at the Bell Buckle Café.

The Chains: Bar-B-Cutie

Known for its iconic images of 1950s cowgirls in short shorts or daring little red skirts representing the restaurant's original carhops, Bar-B-Cutie (bar-b-cutie .com) is a Nashville-based franchise that has been around for quite some time. It started as a 1950s drive-up, carhop-served barbecue restaurant, selling pork sandwiches. It was purchased by the McFarland family in the late 1950s and expanded quickly, adding vegetables and southern-style sides to the menu. As the restaurant grew, they moved from the old Murfreesboro Road location to a larger, all-sit-down place on Nolensville Road. By the mid-1970s, they had opened a drive-through adjacent to the same parking lot as the restaurant that eventually grew to replace its neighbor. A second restaurant appeared on Donelson Pike in 1990. In 2004, the family opted to franchise, and there are now 17 locations across the South (and, believe it or not, two in Spain).

Dolly Parton once waxed poetic to me in an interview about going on dates with her now-husband Carl Thomas Dean at the old Murfreesboro Road location back in the 1960s. For Nashville residents, it's evocative of the city in the mid-20th century at a time when there weren't a whole lot of independent restaurants around, and lots of folks have fond memories.

You can find a franchise in nearly every neighborhood in the city of Nashville and the surrounding area.

While the cafe does great business in burgers, the pulled pork and chicken sandwiches are pretty darned good. On the side, get the spicy fried green beans, although you can't really go wrong with the onion rings either. Then there's a good vinegar slaw (depending on what part of the state you're in vinegar slaw may be served instead of a mayonnaise-based one), pickled beets, white beans and ham, cucumbers, and tomatoes—you can't go wrong.

At dinner, the pork and chicken platters compete with more formal-style meals, including steak and shrimp, as well as pizza, but I'd personally still order them. This is traditional Tennessee pulled pork and chicken served up right, and it's a charming atmosphere. The price is right too, and you can order a pound of barbecue, six buns, and two sides for about $18 to take out.

The cafe offers a banquet hall for events, live music, and plenty of other amenities, but it's also just a perfect place to stop along your drive. For a scenic route, take the back roads down from Murfreesboro.

If you plan a trip down here, come for the Moon Pie Festival in May—you can run the 5K and then really eat with gusto at the cafe.

Big E's Barbecue Restaurant

210 Tommy Dodson Rd., Cookeville, TN 38506; (931) 498-2443; biges bbq.com

Cookeville is a college town, home of Tennessee Tech, and that requires a good joint or two here in the South—Big E's is a favorite for local residents. My friends Mike and Sherry Spivey, who have recently moved to the area from Florida, found it and became addicted almost instantly. "Ernie, the owner, is a great guy," says Mike. "I've had them cater a couple of training days for my business, and everyone has been very happy."

On the menu you start out basic with the pulled pork plate (with or without slaw, make it clear) or the rib plate for a mere $7. Everything here is freshly made, from the smoked meats to the sides. The traditional standbys are all there, and so are the barbecue loaded baked potatoes and the barbecue nachos, including an "all-the-way" version with slaw, cheese, and beans included for those with a solid appetite. You can indeed get a hamburger and also a mesquite grilled chicken sandwich that seems to be a popular choice. Barbecue hot wings and smoked bologna—yes, they have them.

The sides are classics—beans, coleslaw, and potato salad—also available in half-pan sizes to go for a group. Chips, chili, and whole dill pickles round out your options. There's sweet tea, soft drinks, and a cooler of bottled beverages, but don't look for a bar in this location.

As evidenced by Mike's statement above, catering and special event service is readily available. Cookeville is close to several of the state's wineries and a distillery or two. Before you head down to Short Mountain to try real moonshine, makes a stop to fill your stomach at Big E's.

Black Dog Market

6327 Arno Rd., Franklin, TN 37014; (615) 559-5600; facebook.com/
pages/Black-Dog-Market/168991503259910
Live Music Venue

Black Dog Market is out Arno Road in Franklin, easily reached off TN 840. The Arno Road area is beautifully rural and boasts connections to Hatcher Dairy and Delvin Farms, two excellent sources of local milk and produce. If you opt to turn north instead of south off the Arno exit, you'll come to Black Dog Market in just over a mile, conveniently located next to the spot we residents all go to pay our water bills—meaning that's pretty darned convenient to then go in and grab lunch. It bills itself as a convenience store, deli, and barbecue joint, and one of the first things you notice is the huge black smokers off to the side of the unprepossessing wood building.

The vibe is deliberately a bit old country store, the kind that had everything that's gradually been replaced by the minimarts. What's important, however, is that they offer good solid breakfasts (remember this and skip the fast food at the next exit off TN 840) and really good pulled pork sandwiches. On the side, the potato salad and coleslaw are tops. I hesitate to say this about a barbecue joint, but have a slice of their pizza if that's your thing.

There are indoor and outdoor tables if you're one of the many stopping here to grab lunch. Even better, they have not one but two stages inside and regular musical guests if you stop by around dinnertime. Check their Facebook page for updates on who you get to see play as you enjoy your pork sandwich.

Blue Moon Barbecue

711 Park, Lebanon, TN 37087; (615) 444-7920; bluemoonbbqlebanon
.com

Lebanon and the area off I-40 east of Nashville often gets written off by tourists on their way to bigger and better places or identified as "the place with the outlet mall." The outlet mall is all well and good if you need a purse or new running shoes, but skip the fast-food joints up there and get off at exit 239 for Blue Moon. It's a bright, cheerful place, a perfect stop on your cruise along I-40. There are red checked tablecloths, brilliantly painted walls with aged-wood wainscoting, and bicycles hanging from the ceiling.

Owner Todd Beaird smokes his own meat in his own rubs and serves it with house-made sauces. Your smoked meat sandwiches include pork, chicken, brisket, turkey, sausage, and bologna on the daily menu, plus fried catfish served with hushpuppies. You'll also find St. Louis–cut, smoked dry rubbed ribs. You can do a plate with one, two, three, or four meats (extra charge for ribs), which puts a whole different spin on the meat-and-three concept. Those wanting a more traditional route can opt for smoked winged, burgers, and nachos. The Elvis taco showcases a choice of smoked meats on a corn bread tortilla.

They have a plethora of made-in-house side items, including sweet potato waffle fries, mashed redskin potatoes, fried okra, broccoli casserole, and mac and cheese. Buy your banana pudding in large quantities to take home for later if you're too full for dessert. If you're looking to quaff a brew or two, there's a good selection of both domestic and import with which to wash down your sandwich.

To-go and family takeout meals, including whole cuts of meat—whole pork butt and brisket—are readily available. This is a live music locale, so check the website for weekly performers. Closed Monday.

Bobby Q's

482 E. Broad St., Cookeville, TN 38501; (931) 526-1024; facebook.com/pages/Bobby-Qs/140326602653770

Quite aside from the awesomely punny name, Bobby Q's serves up some very solid and delicious barbecue and catfish. Owners Mike and Jane Migliore also pride themselves on their customer service, which is darned good. The interior is full of what seems to be reclaimed barn wood and homey antique touches, like vintage quilts on the wall and old ceramic jugs.

I am at this point required by my friend, Cookeville resident and grad student Heather Murray, to mention that "they're especially known for their amazing banana pudding, no lie." She's right, the banana pudding is worth going for all by itself (of course, you need to eat your meat before pudding, am I right?). As they grind their own coffee, I highly recommend you order some with said pudding.

Bobby's states on the front of their menu that they don't limit themselves to just pork; they'll "barbecue any USDA graded meat or fowl." Take them at their word. The top of that menu jumps you right into pork, ribs, chicken, and beef plates, all served up with bread and a choice of two sides. You can also get fries, curly fries, or baked potato loaded down with barbecue, along with other sides, including green beans, okra, corn on the cob, mac and cheese, and baked sweet potato as well as the usual.

Sweet Treats

It's well known here in the South that we like our sweets, and if you go into most locally owned barbecue joints, let alone small markets, you'll likely see a few treats you've maybe heard of but never tired. The first is the near ubiquitous Moon Pie.

The **Moon Pie** dates to the 1910s, when the Chattanooga Bakery (established 1902), a company that made any number of popular cookies and treats, started producing a delicious little confection of two graham crackers sandwiching a marshmallow filling, dipped in chocolate. The Chattanooga Bakery still makes Moon Pies, and thanks to media references dating back to the golden age of television, they are absolutely linked with the American South. Bell Buckle, Tennessee, hosts a Moon Pie Festival annually, celebrating the Moon Pie and its traditional pairing with RC Cola (a product of Georgia). Eat all the Moon Pies you like at the festival, but make sure you run them off in the event's popular 10K run. Order your Moon Pies at moonpie.com.

Meanwhile, the **Goo-Goo Cluster** may be less well known than the Moon Pie, but it too dominates the popular market here in Tennessee, and it has just celebrated 100 years of production. Starting in 1912, the Standard Candy Company in Nashville started producing these wonderful little masses of calories, with a center of marshmallow nougat, caramel, and roasted peanuts dipped in milk chocolate. Rumor has it the rather unique name came from then owner Howard Campbell Sr.'s infant son—who was learning to talk as the company developed the candy. Order at googoo.com.

Catfish is also a specialty of the house, and it's worth having, even if you reserve the first visit for barbecue. They offer it fried, grilled, or cooked in a mustard sauce and also little catfish bites akin to chicken fingers that will appeal to both adults and kids. These come with homemade hushpuppies, by the way.

As is to be expected, catering and event service is available.

Bubba's Smokehouse

1029 West College St., Pulaski, TN 38478; facebook.com/bubbas
.smokehouse.tn

Another of the winning small barbecue joints, this one is down in Pulaski, almost on the Alabama border. The sign outside reads "nuttin' butt good"— punning on the exceptional quality of the pork butts they marinate and cook for hours on end over their own custom blend of hardwoods. Enjoy the pun, enjoy the menu. The super nice staff doesn't do any harm either. Start out with barbecue nachos or chili cheese nachos or, if your appetite is lighter, maybe a barbecue wrap (pork or chicken).

Bubba's has a really good selection of meats—the usual pork dominance, but don't neglect pulled chicken, beef brisket, or barbecue "baloney" when you think about your order. Choose from St. Louis–style or baby back ribs, depending on your whim.

The slaw menu should be captioned "some like it hot" with its hot mustard and spicy vinegar variations (there is a creamy mayo for the faint of palate). The white beans are particularly good, and as the menu tells you, try them with corn bread.

The specials are ridiculously inexpensive, including a good option for your Monday lunch, with two pork sandwiches for $4, cheaper than a loaded fast-food burger from a drive-through (Bubba's has a drive-through, no worries, just better than fast food). Among the special options are loaded baked potatoes, homemade soups, and fresh pies on the dessert menu as well as de rigeur banana pudding.

Follow the Facebook page for daily specials—the prices are terribly low for such good food, but Pulaski is home to Martin Methodist College, and this definitely appeals to every college student around. Catering is available. Closed Sunday.

Carl's Perfect Pig Bar-B-Que and Grill

4991 E. US 70, White Bluff, TN 37187; (615) 797-4020; carlsperfectpig
.com

White Bluff, Tennessee, might be a little off the beaten track, but if you're driving along I-40 around Dickson, it's really less than 15 minutes out of your way
to make the stop. This place is pretty legendary among local barbecue lovers.
The hours aren't conductive to a long, leisurely dinner, but the food is *so* worth
it. Both pork and beef are on the menu, and, frankly, you probably want to get
some ribs if you haven't been here before. My friend Carson Reed introduced
me to this place, and I've never regretted the discovery.

The owners started Carl's to escape from the mid-century turn away from
traditional pit barbecue in this part of the state—a lot of the best joints got
started that way. Rejecting the conventional oven, they committed themselves
to doing real, old-school barbecue, and the results can't be argued with.

If you are ordering the pork, go ahead and get it on the corn cake instead
of a bun—it's a very Middle Tennessee thing, and it's really smashing—you'll
love the flavor combination. They also take their sides seriously, but be aware
that the ribs are generally ordered with fries—and be okay with that choice, as
they're good fries.

You can get plenty of classic meat-and-three southern foods here—hand-
breaded chicken livers (yes, they're terrific), grilled turkey, a pretty good jalapeño burger, catfish, and even a steak—but people come here mostly for the
barbecue and the ribs. Save some room for the banana pudding; it's some of
the best in the state.

Carl's melds the best of old and new in the barbecue world—it's got an old-
school philosophy and a tucked-away location set out in the middle of a small
town, not in the heart of Nashville or Memphis. But they pride themselves on
cooking barbecue right, and you can't argue with the food you get.

If they're old school, they also buy into social media very effectively—the
daily specials are posted on the restaurant's Facebook page at facebook.com/
CarlsPerfectPigWB. And, by the way, they cater and do weddings. Closed
Monday and Tuesday.

Center Point

1212 W. Main St., Hendersonville, TN 37075; (615) 824-9330; center
pointbbq.com

You probably saw Center Point on *Drive Ins, Diners and Dives,* and the Sumner
County location deserved its television promotion quite thoroughly. Calling
themselves the "home of the Three Little Pigs," Center Point does pretty much

everything right. Hendersonville and Gallatin, just north of Nashville in Sumner County, get lumped into metro Nashville a lot, but really they have a food culture all their own. Center Point is a good example.

There are plenty of old-fashioned Middle Tennessee specialties on the menu, along with barbecue—look for fried squash and fried green tomatoes on the appetizers menu. You can get your barbecue pulled or minced the way they do in Carolina, and there's no wrong answer (I like pulled, myself). This is the kind of place you come for a real rib sandwich, that fast-food chain notwithstanding. Look for hickory-smoked hot sausages as a great alternative barbecue here, and don't be afraid to order your barbecue on corn bread, the way they do it around here.

There are three different slaws. I like mine spicy and red, but there's a creamy mayo for traditionalists and a vinegar based option as well. Also consider the white beans and onions on the side.

They advertise "the world's best homemade barbecue sauce"—seriously, it's pretty darned good.

There's no bar, but the drink menu includes buttermilk and local grapefruit soda Sundrop (loaded with caffeine, too). Family packs are available as takeout only, and catering is available.

Center Point has been around for more than 40 years now for a good reason—the barbecue is worth coming back for, to say the least.

Christie Q Barbecue and Catering

28 Hummingbird Ln., Woodbury, TN 37190; (615) 785-0206; facebook
.com/pages/Christie-Q-Bbq-and-Catering/332118146809175

Mike and Christie Alexander have helped spread the food truck trend beyond the larger metropolitan hubs and out into the area around Woodbury, Sparta, and McMinnville. Their distinctive bright pink truck, with its pig-in-a-bib logo, is an indication you've come to a good place. The barbecue game is a sideline for them, but they've been very successful catering events all over the state, from Pulaski to Lookout Mountain on the Georgia border. You can find the food truck out and about on Friday and Saturday mostly in the area from Woodbury east to Sparta or west to Murfreesboro—often in the Tractor Supply parking lots.

"We'll travel anywhere," Mike says cheerfully. They're about spreading the gospel of "basic barbecue" that's really anything but basic. They offer up brisket, pulled pork, award-winning ribs, chicken, and especially good wings. The smoked bologna, which gets a specially crafted rub, plus Mike's special glaze post-smoking, is served up with his own take on Alabama white sauce and is a thing of beauty.

The meats are smoked on all wood, cherry, hickory, and persimmon. "It's a heavy kind of smoke, but it gives good flavor," says Mike. Christie Q makes all their own sauces, the locally popular sweet and hot, plus the above-mentioned white, a Carolina-style vinegar sauce, and a wasabi honey sauce, "kind of like a supped up honey mustard" they use for half chickens and the like. Like most Tennesseans, the sweet and sweet-hot are the sauces that go over best around Woodbury.

On the side, check out the huge loaded baked potato, heavy with pork and chicken (or make it a meal). Also look for barbecue beans, coleslaw, great green beans like your grandma used to make, and the new loaded baked potato salad. Mike recommends the corn bread salad—"it's redneck healthy"—with pinto and white beans, niblet corn, tomatoes, green onions, radishes, bacon, and a mix of ranch and Alabama white sauce.

For dessert—cobbler or the Christie Cake—a wonder of German Chocolate filled with coconut and cream cheese, topped with candy bars and a deep chocolate glaze guaranteed to please any chocoholic around.

Christie Q caters events without the truck, but they'll happily bring it to family get-togethers, parties, civic meetings, and other events as well. Open Friday and Saturday only, plus special events.

Collins River BBQ

117 E. Main St., McMinnville, TN 37110; (931) 507-3663; facebook .com/pages/Collins-River-BBQ-Cafe/172711612810036
McMinnville is one of the those areas, on the fringe between Middle and East Tennessee, served by any number of the little shack-type joints that change names but always seem to be there. Collins River BBQ, named for one of the three rivers that converge just west of town and owned by the local O'Neil family, is the town's recent answer to the demand for something a little more sophisticated, though the food is good old-fashioned Tennessee barbecue. The locals must love the place because they won the 2014 Best of Warren County Award rather easily. It's set in an old drugstore in the historic downtown that's been converted, showcasing a big stage and old brick walls. (Note: There are sometimes cover charges on nights with a big music program.)

On the menu are classic barbecue sandwiches (both pork and brisket), pork ribs, and a variety of custom sandwiches, and the smoked wings make the most popular starter here. Don't look for huge portion sizes, especially with sides, as one serving will feed one person (not a bad thing). There are local beers on tap, including Calfkiller, made in nearby Sparta, Tennessee—always a plus in my book. Sauces are good, and the sides include some pretty good

The Chains: Dickey's Barbecue Pit

Dickey's (dickeys.com) is another chain making its way into Tennessee, Kentucky, and Alabama, with locations in Brentwood and Clarksville, Tennessee, and Huntsville, Alabama, among others. Given its popularity, I'd expect to see more by the time this book has been out for a year or so.

The first Dickey's opened in Dallas, Texas, in 1941—which pretty much tells you this will be more Texas-style barbecue than Tennessee/Alabama. His adult sons took the business over in 1967 and made serious effort to retain the classic styles their father had pioneered with his hickory-smoked barbecue. Over time, the restaurant expanded to new locations across the Dallas–Fort Worth area. In 1994, the company began franchising and expanded into this region.

The menu offers smoked pulled pork, beef brisket, and less typical options, like barbecue honey ham and cheddar sausage, as well as ribs, turkey, and chicken. Side options include jalapeño beans, coleslaw, mac and cheese, and a baked potato casserole. Both catering and takeout are readily available. The franchise is known for their popular pecan pie, plus free ice cream and buttery rolls with your meal.

sweet potatoes, baked beans, mac and cheese, and the like. Barbecue nachos, barbecue salads, and an intriguing brisket BLT round out the menu.

Last time I was in, they were preparing to close the restaurant for a week so they could run things from a booth at the Warren County Fair. The restaurant also offers catering for events large and small, including weddings.

Corner Pit BBQ

Dellrose Rd., Bryson, TN; (931) 732-4575; cornerpitbbq.com

Clay Cutler at Tenn South Distillery insisted I include this particular location. Corner Pit BBQ lives just off exit 6 on I-65 south, almost in North Alabama. Your GPS may say it's in Pulaski, but don't believe it. The correct answer is Bryson, Tennessee. The unprepossessing wooden building has been a barbecue joint since the mid-1960s, when it was Russell's Barbecue under the direction of Willard Russell and his wife, Geraldine. When they retired, they sold it to the Burnham family, who in turn sold it in 1997 to Bo and Jane Witt. Over the years, the takeout barbecue pit has acquired some indoor seating and became a true restaurant. In 2008, Bill and Krysten Pfeiffer bought the place, revamped it after a fire had wrecked the pits prior to their purchase, and reopened. Locals and travelers alike make regular visits.

Pulled pork, brisket, and ribs dominate the menu. Look to the ¼-¼ Special for a terrific blend of pork and brisket on one sandwich. You'll also find barbecue chicken, chicken sandwiches, rib tips, and hamburgers on the menu for diversity and all the standard sides, plus some good Brunswick stew. As is usual with these places, pints and quarts of sides and bulk meat purchase are available for you to take home, and yes indeed, they cater.

It may not be the flashiest joint you eat at on your barbecue sojourn in Tennessee, but it will definitely be a favorite.

It isn't advertised on the signs for exit 6, which are dominated by fast food and the like, but turn right from the exit, drive right past it all for 2 miles, and you'll find your way to good local barbecue.

Edley's Bar-B-Que

908 Main St., Nashville, TN 37206, (615) 873-4085; 2706 12th Ave. S., Nashville, TN 37204 (East Nashville), (615) 953-2951; edleysbbq.com

Brett Newman, a native of McMinnville, Tennessee, really dreamed up the notion of opening a barbecue restaurant with his wife, Catharine. She's from Birmingham, and it was actually North Alabama's take on what we consider classic Tennessee style that inspired them. Both Edley's locations are cool and inviting—perfectly suited to the 12 Avenue South and East Nashville

neighborhoods they are set in—and offsetting a good bit of upscale-style cuisine sold at the places around them. The restaurant is a good solid blend of the meat-and-three concept (meaning you should rightfully have high expectations for marvelous side items) and traditional barbecue places.

Edley's is ideally placed as a lunch spot for the business crowd, but it draws in plenty of families come dinnertime. There are myriad daily specials (check the board), and Edley's does some fun things—like the East Nashville location's periodic catfish fry. But it still comes down to the fact that they smoke truly good meats and blend that with the region's meat-and-three tradition to make a righteous meal.

You have to try the pork—it's the foundation of what makes the restaurant worth visiting, but you'll also want to try the smoked turkey sandwich because, as Catharine Newman puts it, it's "sneaky good." They do smoke a bit of brisket—available at lunch only—and it's delicious. Also worth a trip back are the smoked chicken wings—if you're a wing fan, you need to try them.

Just about the only thing not made in-house is desert, but they're made locally by Colt's Chocolates. The bar is a thing of beauty, with beer, a solid list of bourbon and whiskey, and moonshine cocktails, like the Moon-a-rita and the Moon-jito. All 16 beers on tap are southern in origin, though national brands can be had in bottles.

It very much meets the Nashville zeitgeist, with barn wood and tin, an expansive patio, and an extensive bar—and that just makes your visit even more enjoyable.

Edz Wingz

501 Oak St., Fayetteville, TN 37334; (931) 433-9424; edzwingz.com

My good friend and fellow costumer Jennifer Matthews and I spend a good deal of time in Fayetteville, Tennessee, because it's home to the epically huge Sir's Fabrics—a Mecca for anyone in the state who sews. We tend to make a day of it and head down early in the morning, shop, grab lunch, and shop some more. This is where Edz comes in.

It's a sports bar with some barbecue leanings, but Edz "Short Bus Barbecue Crew" keeps the pork butts, Texas-style beef brisket, and Memphis-inspired ribs flowing throughout the "barbecue season," sometimes selling outdoors from their converted mini school bus. Fortunately, barbecue season seems to coincide nicely with baseball and football season, and Edz is prepared for that reality as well, with plenty of televisions tuned to SEC games and a steady supply of cold beer and beverage specials. If your taste runs to Carolina-style barbecue sauce, you're in real luck because Edz serves up locally made Harold's Hog Wash barbecue sauce (order at haroldshogwash .com; it has received praise from plenty of local sources as well as larger outlets, like *Southern Living*).

Edz's real specialty is wings, and those are there all year long. There's a vast assortment of wing sauces, fear not, if your tastes run to things like honey mustard or teriyaki instead of classic barbecue. On the menu, you'll also find good burgers, hot dogs, and assorted sandwiches, salads for those so inclined, and darned good chili. Remember where I said sports bar—that's your guideline here; the only thing that keeps it from being an ideal specimen is a lack of local microbrew. But the wings and barbecue make even a losing game better. Closed Sunday and Monday.

Excell Market and Barbecue

3102 Ashland City Rd., Clarksville, TN 37043; (931) 358-3638

I had never heard of Excell until my friend, local food specialist Melissa Corbin (corbininthedell.com), mentioned it to me. One thing I've learned over the past year or so of knowing her is that if she says "go try this place," you go and try it. She was not wrong, as they make a darned good pork sandwich.

Excell is set in a former gas station in Clarksville, not too far from Fort Campbell, and if you're expecting the bright and shining interiors that have become typical in the immediate Nashville area, forget it. What you will get is very good barbecue, and that's what this is all about.

The meat doesn't have an overwhelmingly smoky flavor, but that's not a negative. Order a pork sandwich, and you'll be pleased. The sauce has a distinct vinegar quality that is a little more North Carolina than is typical in Middle Tennessee, with less vinegar than might be used in Carolina. The ribs are fairly solid examples as well.

Excell underlines the reality that you have to look past the visual in the vast majority of places you stop in the state of Tennessee that are outside major metro areas and just enjoy what you find.

Middle Tennessee Travel

Middle Tennessee is hot right now on a national level. If you're looking for something to do, there's plenty out there, but here are a few favorites that won't disappoint you when planning a visit.

Cheekwood (1200 Forrest Park Dr., Nashville, TN 37205; cheekwood.org)—With lush botanical gardens and a glorious mid-19th-century mansion filled with art, Cheekwood is a family outing not to be missed. You can spend an entire day just exploring the grounds, whatever the season. There's always an outdoor exhibit—recent options include Trains! (an interactive experience with a kid-friendly focus) and the art of Dale Chihuly.

Downtown Franklin (Main St., Franklin, TN 37064; downtownfranklintn .com)—This charming historic small town just south of Nashville proper offers up an exquisite antiques district off Second Avenue, a walkable downtown full of locally owned boutiques and shops, and several major historic sites, including the **Carter House,** the **Lotz House,** and **Carnton Plantation.** Plan to spend a whole day here shopping, eating, and exploring.

PHOTO COURTESY OF MAGGIE JACKSON, CHEEKWOOD

Downtown Murfreesboro (downtownmurfreesboro.com)—A hidden gem of a historic courthouse crowns the square in downtown Murfreesboro, with locally owned shops in buildings dating to the very early 19th century. Nearby, visit **MTSU's Heritage Center** (225 W. College St., Murfreesboro, TN 37130) or take a walk at the **Stones River Battlefield.**

The Frist Center for the Visual Arts (919 Broadway, Nashville, TN 37203; fristcenter.org)—Although the museum has been around less than a decade, you can be sure there's an extraordinary show or two going on any time you visit. Set in the old art deco–style downtown post office (yes, there's still a post office inside), this gorgeous museum has something for parents and children alike and plenty of interactive exhibits.

Nashville Zoo at Grassmere (nashvillezoo.org)—Always the perfect family spot, the Nashville Zoo has a plethora of new exhibits to wow kids and adults, from otters to flamingos to giraffes. More than 300 different species can be observed on any visit, the locale is beautiful, and it's just a grand day out in the city.

State Parks and Recreation Areas—While you're here, don't forget Middle Tennessee's abundance of outdoor recreation areas and state parks, many with lakes suitable for swimming and boating. Among the favorites are **Fall Creek Falls State Park, Rock Island State Park, Tim's Ford State Park, Center Hill Lake,** and **Percy Priest Lake.**

Fat Boys Bar-B-Q

2733 Murfreesboro Pike, Nashville, TN 37013; (615) 360-9969; fatboys
barbq.com

"We are a 'joint,'" says owner Tony Roney of the place he opened in 2009 with
the help of his sister Cara Salamy. They had never had a restaurant before, and
they called on the barbecue lessons taught by their late uncle and a plethora
of scrumptious recipes from a variety of family members. The cozy little place
may not be fancy—simple tables and chairs, uplifting Scripture on a board on
the wall, and a hodgepodge of mismatched funky objects—but the food is terrific, and the service shines.

The barbecue uses a dry rub and is cooked over hickory, with the ribs
and brisket winning the customer popularity contest. All sauces are served
on the side. The creamy mac and cheese—pure cheese, butter, and milk—is
number one in customer eyes for sides, with the Powerhouse Beans (redolent
with hamburger and onion), old-fashioned turnip greens, and fried corn bread
following suit.

Fat Boys also has Nashville-staple hot chicken (chicken fried with a thick
paste of truly hot spices, dominated by cayenne), and customers come in
almost as often for the fried catfish and whiting as they do for the barbecue.

When it comes to dessert? Aim for chess squares, big servings of ever-
present banana pudding, brownies, or bread pudding. Sweet Tea and soda have
always been on the menu, but unsweetened tea has recently appeared. "When
people asked, I just said, 'We're called Fat Boys, everything on the menu has
either pork or sugar,'" says Cara with a laugh. Closed Sunday.

Grandpa's Tennessee Barbecue

2390 Depot St., Spring Hill, TN 37174; (615) 290-4208; facebook.com/
pages/Grandpas-Tennessee-Barbeque/197093563783809

Grandpa's is the new barbecue business in town for Spring Hill residents, but
the trick is that they're open only Thursday through Saturday. In Middle Tennessee, where folks are used to having 7-day-a-week service on everything,
that's unusual. Owner Richard Terry wears several hats, from barbecue cook to
ordained preacher, and he loves cooking up ribs for his customers.

The options from Grandpa's are small and specific—choose from pulled
pork, ribs, and brisket, with a minimum order of 2 pounds, and pick up or have
it delivered. The business promises to have smoked turkey available come
Thanksgiving as well. What makes it all particularly good are the homemade
rubs (there are four that Terry makes himself) and handcrafted sauces, with a
choice of sweet or spicy.

Grandpa's doesn't appear to be a first business for Terry. Instead, he and his wife just like cooking barbecue, and they keep a handle on their needs by asking for preorders and smoking only a few days a week—not trying to open a large-scale joint (I thought Spring Hill is a rapidly growing community, and there's no doubt there's room for that in future if they decide to take things bigger). For now, it's the place locals go to get something truly good that tastes of home. Closed Sunday through Wednesday.

Heavenly BarB-Que

7923 Tullahoma Hwy., Estill Springs, TN 37330; (931) 649-5767

This is a place I know of courtesy of my Sewanee friend Jennifer Matthews, who will tell anyone who asks that this is the best place for pulled pork in the area. The painted cinder-block building with wide picture windows announces itself with a sign featuring winged and haloed hogs underlining just how "heavenly" the food really is here. It's a roadside stop, one of the best of its kind in this area, but don't look for fancy or formal, just good old casual.

You'll find beef, chicken, and ribs in addition to the pulled pork, but if you haven't learned by now that when pulled pork is the house specialty, you order it, then you just haven't learned. The sampler on the menu allows you to try a bit of everything, so if you're adventurous, that's no bad start either. You'll find all the usual side suspects and a few atypical ones—the loaded twice-baked potato salad regularly gets raves from the patrons.

The atmosphere is warm, the food is good, takeout is available, and service is friendly.

Hog Heaven

115 27th Ave. N., Nashville, TN 37203; (615) 329-1234; hogheavenbbq .com

Set next to Centennial Park, just off the Vanderbilt campus and right next door to a big-chain fast-food restaurant, Hog Heaven's little wooden building with the smokers out back seems somewhat incongruous, especially along fast-paced West End Avenue less than half a block down. The thing is that it's not unusual to see the bespectacled professors, jeans-clad students, and business-dressed professionals lining up for lunch at the tiny place. It may not have the high-end atmosphere, but it sure has the food worth the wait.

Most of the seating is outdoors—everything is takeout from the counter. In fine weather, you find patrons spilling across the vast greens of the park toward the huge replica of the Parthenon that stands there. Order yourself a sandwich of hand-pulled pork, chicken, brisket, or turkey with a side of coleslaw, mac and cheese, or beans. The red sauce is tangy and delicious (they default to an Alabama-style white sauce on the chicken, also yummy). For dessert, follow your meal with homemade peach or blackberry cobbler.

My friends with small children say this place pleases their kids pretty well, and that's a great sign if you have the family along on your trip.

As it happens, you can take home a pound of barbecue at a good price, and if you want spareribs, they have good ones. There is soda but no beer or liquor.

Hog Heaven has received a lot of national publicity of late from the likes of the Food Network (*The Best Thing I Ever Ate*), *Southern Living*, the Travel Channel, and others—but it's deserved praise, and the publicity hasn't done anything to change the friendly attitude or the longtime quality of the food. If you're on the West End, skip the dozens of chains at lunch and find Hog Heaven. You'll have no cause for regret and a restaurant you will always willingly return to given the chance. Closed Sunday.

Jack's BarBQue

416 Broadway, Nashville, TN 37203, (615) 254-5715; 334 West Trinity Ln., Nashville, TN 37207, (615) 228-9888; 1601 Charlotte Ave., Nashville, TN 37203, (615) 341-0157; jacksbarbeque.com

For the longest time, the name "Jack's" equaled Nashville barbecue; back years ago, when Jack Cawthon started out, barbecue in Nashville was limited in its scope. Cawthon got his start in a tiny building on the corner of First Avenue and Broadway before the downtown area was renovated and truly became the haunt of tourists and visitors. But the food was good, and not only locals but tourists started flocking in. Today, the downtown Jack's is a landmark (and its sign, a city icon), but it has moved down the street, smack on Broadway and holding far more people than ever managed to fit in the small original. It's the location most tourists flock to (and for good reason, as the food's good, and sometimes the lines are long). But if you head out to Charlotte Avenue or West Trinity, the crowds are a bit lighter, it's easier to get a seat, and the menu remains the same.

Jack's Original sauces have won myriad prizes over the years. I tend to favor the sweet-hot sauce, I must admit. Catering and bulk orders are available, and you can order the sauces and dry rubs from the website. On the first visit, get the Tennessee Pork Shoulder sandwich with some coleslaw and baked beans or mac and cheese—it's pretty straightforward. On the next trip, branch out a little to try the smoked turkey breast or the sausage. You're in Nashville, so finish up with chess pie for heaven's sake.

The Broadway and Charlotte Pike locations offer beer, and both also have a patio, as luck would have it.

Jim N' Nick's

7004 Charlotte Pike, Nashville, TN 37209, (615) 352-5777; 3068 Mallory Ln., Franklin, TN 37067, (615) 771-3939; 523 Sam Ridley Pkwy. W., Smyrna, TN 37167, (615) 220-8508; 436 N. Thompson Ln., Murfreesboro, TN 37129, (615) 893-1001; jimnnicks.com

Okay, okay, Jim n' Nick's is a chain (see also the section "North Alabama"), but it's not your typical chain. In part, that's because founder Nick Pihakis remains so involved in his company and shares his philosophy and his community-serving spirit along with his recipes and methods. In part, it's because unlike the vast majority of the chains out there, Jim N' Nick's feels like it belongs, wherever you go in.

Local owner Molly James not only owns several of the franchises but also has done her time at the pit and knows how to make a difference in the way barbecue is prepared all on her own. Molly is a power house part of the Middle Tennessee barbecue community, and to leave out her restaurants because they're part of a chain would be a disservice.

PHOTO COURTESY OF NICK PIHAKIS, JIM N' NICK'S BBQ

The menu brims with protein offerings (as Nick says, it makes sure there's no "veto vote" when folks go out), and there's always something to please anyone walking in the door. Chicken and turkey breast arrive in Alabama white sauce, tangy and delicious. The baby back ribs are juicy, and the pork—whether Tennessee/Alabama pulled style or Carolina chopped (yes, you can get both)—is sure to please. You could do worse than start out as a group and share the BBQ nachos. For those who want them, there are more standard-fare burgers and sandwiches too.

For dessert, the pies—like everything else—are made fresh in the restaurant each day. Go for the Coconut Cream or the Pecan. There's definitely a bar, and beer, wine, and quite luscious cocktails can all be had, assuming you're of age. I have to admit that sometimes the girl drinks at the bar here are just what the doctor ordered if you want a little barbecue on a girls' night.

You can order Jim N' Nick's signature sauces and more online, and I highly recommend it.

Jim N' Nick's and Nick Pihakis

It's nearly impossible to write about Jim N' Nick's as a chain because the word "chain" carries its own implications—often of prefab, microwaved food, and dull atmosphere—and anyone who has met Nick Pihakis understands that his dedication to not only the restaurant business but barbecue itself remains extraordinary nearly three decades in and keeps Jim N' Nick's from ever being ordinary.

Nick started with a background in the restaurant business, and his dad Jim came from the insurance world. Together, they decided to make use of the best of both sets of acumen and start a barbecue restaurant. At the end of the 20th century, Nick reflects in conversation, barbecue in Alabama—and all over the region—was in an odd place. Barbecue tends to be a generational thing, passed on from parents to children, and at that juncture, more second and third generations were opting to move on from small-scale family operations. Likewise, there was an opening in the market, and Jim N' Nick's first store in Birmingham met that need. These days, Nick's own son is also involved with the business.

Over time, Jim N' Nick's has grown from the single restaurant where Nick learned to smoke barbecue with the aid of one of the old pitmasters from Birmingham's famed Ollie's barbecue restaurant and which started by serving just pork and chicken, baked beans, slaw, fries, and onion rings to a small chain of more than 30 locations. All of them remain tightly tied to Nick's philosophy—not only of food and southern foodways but of giving back to the community as a whole.

He has been recognized by the James Beard Foundation as a semifinalist for outstanding restaurateur in the region for the past 4 years running, but beyond that, he has also supported up-and-coming barbecue chefs, like Patrick Martin in Nashville, and committed himself to helping rebuild farming networks in the region through the Fatback Collective (see the section "The Outliers").

Jim N' Nick's itself offers up a broad diversity of proteins—there's absolutely something on the menu for everyone, whether you want classic pulled

(continued)

pork or ribs, smoked turkey, or really just a burger. The goal is to take nothing for granted. Meats are cooked over an open fire of hickory wood (no charcoal); everything is made fresh daily (no freezers).

While there's a good family menu, there's also a bar, and beer, wine, and cocktails are available—frequently spectacular original signature cocktails. The atmosphere welcomes; it's the kind of place you want to come back to repeatedly. And that's as Nick Pihakis intended.

John T's BBQ Smokehouse

115 First Ave NE, Winchester, TN 37398; (931) 967-9600; johntbbq .com

I have a lot of friends who live in Sewanee, and while Sewanee has many things, including the University of the South, what it doesn't have lots of is barbecue. Fortunately, nearby Winchester provides other options. The rumor is that John T's is the best option in the area for ribs, and the people who say that among my friends have reason to be in the know. Set in a charming old brick building with memorabilia on the walls, live music on a regular basis, and a general good atmosphere—not to mention draft beer—John T's makes for a reason to visit Winchester (it's not too far from Jack Daniel's and George Dickel either if you've been touring and need a good dinner).

The menu offers up some trendy southern bits—fried green tomatoes as a starter, for example—but is dominated by good, solid Tennessee barbecue (yes, even the brisket proclaims that it's "Tennessee style"). Order ribs on your first visit, but if you're looking other directions, pork shoulder, smoked chicken halves, wings, the preciously remarked-on brisket, plus burgers and fried catfish mean there are plenty of options. The side items include turnip greens, hoecakes, white beans, and spicy buffalo fries along with the usuals.

Barbecue nachos and baked potatoes do indeed make their way to the menu, and the "Meat Dinner Salad" is a solid take on the barbecue salad trend.

You absolutely must save room for dessert—the banana pudding is very good, and there's always a cobbler of the day worth trying.

Yes, there is a drive-through (call ahead, it helps!). Bulk meat and side orders are also available for takeout. Visit the website for a current music calendar to see who's playing on the day of your visit.

Judge Bean's BBQ

7022 Church St. E., Brentwood, TN 37027; (615) 823-2280; judge beans.com

Judge Bean's has been Texas barbecue's best incarnation in the Nashville area for well over a decade. I've interviewed founder Aubrey Bean on his ventures numerous times, starting at the charming place he used to have downtown in a century-old building across from 12th and Porter that was reputed to be haunted. His original place was on Wedgewood, over by the state fairgrounds near Berry Hill (where he's recently opened yet another incarnation).

Bean sold his Brentwood place to partners after some health concerns a few years ago (he opened The Vinegaroon downtown shortly afterward but closed it in September 2014—even so, when he opens anything, the barbecue lovers in town take notice). It still offers his take on Texas barbecue, and he should be credited for it. Around lunchtime, this Brentwood locale is packed with business traffic. (Word to the wise: Order to go, even if there's no drive-through.)

Its being Texas style, it's easy to recommend the brisket, but both the smokehouse ribs and the smoked chicken deserve consideration on the menu. The place has always offered superb smoked wings, which work either as a starter or as a meal, and, frankly, the smoky salsa served with chips is unlike the other iterations you find around here.

There are plenty of side options; I tend to go with fries here because they're very good. Gluttons for caloric punishment can probably see their way to the chili cheese fries. Catering and takeout are available and remain very popular during football season for that reason.

Larry's Bar-B-Que

1941 Dercherd Blvd., Dercherd, TN; (931) 967-9163; facebook.com/pages/Larrys-Bar-B-Que/136155723106744

Larry's makes no pretentions about being anything other than a barbecue joint, with its brightly decorated deck and casual atmosphere. It's cozy, kitschy, and covered with vintage-style signs. You can grab food to go or have a seat and dine, but either way, look out for some mighty good ribs and pork. In moderate weather, out on the deck is kind of the place to be—and that's good because inside there aren't a whole lot of tables. As you drive along, look for the painted concrete pig—it's a dead giveaway you're in the right place.

The menu is simple and easy to pick from—get a good sandwich—pork (Boston butt), chicken, or beef—or choose the ribs. Your side options include the beans, slaw, and potato salad but also macaroni and pasta salads, green beans, turnip greens, and corn on the cob. Family packs and other carryouts are available. This is another place where you want to maintain at least a little room at the end of the meal for one of the superb homemade pies that come out of the kitchen. (I should tell of cookies as well, but I never make it past the pie.)

The prices are very reasonable, and this is also a spot that makes for an easy drive over from the big distilleries if you're making a day of it. Closed Sunday.

Martin's Bar-B-Que Joint

7238 Nolensville Rd., Nolensville, TN 37135, (615) 776-1856; 3108 Belmont Blvd., Nashville, TN 37212, (615) 200-1181; 2200 Crossings Ln., Mount Juliet, TN 37122, (615) 686-2066; martinsbbqjoint.com

With brand-new additional locations in Mount Juliet (2200 Crossings Ln.) and in the Belmont neighborhood (3108 Belmont Blvd.), it's still wrong to confuse Martin's with a chain restaurant. Owner Patrick Martin trains all his managers himself, and there's a consistency across all three spots that few restaurants manage. Also consistent are the long lines and lunch and dinner—because the food is just that good. Fortuitously, they move fast, and there's a drive thru.

Pat's smokers are out in the open, and if you're lucky, you can observe the hog being cooked (he also cooks shoulders and butts, but a couple of times a week, whole hog is on the menu). Children of locals are completely fascinated by the ritual opening of the in-house pit, and you'll often see them with parents, sitting along the edge looking over into it while they eat.

You honestly can't go wrong with this menu, but on your first visit, just order the pork sandwich. Next time, branch out to the redneck taco—barbecue served on a corn bread hoecake (a very Middle Tennessee thing) with seriously good slaw. And I hate to admit it, but the best chicken tenders in town are here too. Yeah, really—order them with the Alabama white sauce. Also on the menu is the smoked bologna, which, if bologna is your thing, can't be beat.

Pat grew up in West Tennessee whole hog–cooking country, he's passionate about it, and he's something of a whole hog evangelist. He's been taking his philosophy on the road to Big Apple Barbecue and Charleston Food and Wine for several years now, but he's still an old-school barbecue guy.

The vibe is very Middle Tennessee—barn wood walls, garage doors, and Pat's own super-eclectic music mixes (from AC/DC to Merle Haggard). Order a beer at the bar—there are lots of southern microbrews on tap. (Full disclosure: I'm the blonde girl in the Jack Daniel's T-shirt on the reruns of *Drive-Ins, Diners, and Dives* talking up the barbecue here with Guy Fieri. They catered my wedding, I like them that much—and I'm here at least weekly.)

I love Martin's. If I don't eat here frequently, I have withdrawal. I am not alone in this feeling, trust me.

Mickey Roos

509 Hillsboro Rd., Franklin, TN 37064; (615) 599-5993; mickeyroos .com

Mickey Roos is more a Texas-style place with Tennessee elements than true Tennessee barbecue, but it's worth a visit if you're in the Franklin area. They have some pretty good shows—although in Tennessee, the likelihood of a popular food emporium having very good live music is higher than average, by far. There's an appealing bar atmosphere—and plenty of beer options and attractive servers—and the food is worth coming in for, even if you don't care about the evening's band. (And the music is usually worth hearing.)

Start your meal with the fried pickles or some smoked wings—something Mickey Roos does very well. The follow-up should be a brisket sandwich, while the brave of heart might want to risk the Texas Style Heart Attack sandwich, which piles on the brisket, pork, and sausage all together. There are also a few Tex-Mex options on the menu, but a barbecue purist will probably like the sandwiches best. Slow-smoked pork ribs make an excellent meal here as well. The sides include some spicy hot beans (and a mild variation of these), onion rings, fried okra, fries, and corn on the cob. For dessert, follow up all that heat with some creamy Blue Bell ice cream, and you'll be soothed and happy.

Barbecue by the pound is readily available, and Mickey Roos will cater everything from big parties to tailgating events. If you haven't figured out that barbecue and tailgating are practically synonymous in the region, now is the time to make that connection.

I first discovered this place while editor of a local magazine—they were advertising, and I was encouraged to write about them—and it proved one of those places worth coming back to after all the writing was over.

The Chains: Moe's Original

Moe's Original has recently started to pop up across Tennessee and Alabama. While the franchise has its origins with a trio from Tuscaloosa, Alabama, it actually started in Colorado. So, while it's southern style, it truly is also filtered through the viewpoint of the West.

The founders, Ben Gilbert, Jeff Kennedy, and Mike Fernandez, were born and raised in North Alabama and met while attending the University of Alabama at Tuscaloosa. Fernandez developed his interest in barbecue then and learned the art of barbecue cooking from a local master of the craft. When the trio found themselves living in Vail, Colorado, a few years later, they revisited their love for the genre, developed some sauces, and had a concept, though all were in separate restaurant venues. In 2001, they began smoking meats together and then catering in Minturn, just outside Vail.

Their success with the barbecue catering led in turn to their building a barbecue concession trailer aimed at summer tourism, selling out daily at their spot in Edwards, Colorado, for 3 consecutive summers. That success was followed by a carryout venture in Vail's Lionshead Village during the ski season starting in 2002—Moe's Original Lionshead Tin Top morphed into a real little restaurant in 2004. In 2003, they also added a place at the nearby Beaver Creek Resort.

(This is the point where my family and I, coming out to ski regularly at Vail, first discovered them. To quote my dad, "This is pretty good for something you got in Colorado." We weren't remotely aware that the guys behind it were from Alabama and knew the region's cookery. Conveniently, we can now get our "Vail barbecue" in Franklin, Tennessee.)

In 2005, they opened a restaurant in Eagle, Colorado, and then began expanding back to home, in Alabama, with locations in Orange Beach and Birmingham, and then gradually across both states. They now have locations in North Carolina, Georgia, Maine, Tennessee, Ohio, Florida, and now South Carolina.

For all their interesting geography, Moe's produces a sandwich that very much reflects Tennessee and North Alabama and should be counted as regional, even if they did start out in the wilds of Colorado.

O'Possum's Pub

2341 Memorial Blvd., Murfreesboro, TN 37130; (615) 567-5757; opossumspub.com; facebook.com/Opossums

O'Possum's is many things, and its claim to fame is as an Irish-style watering hole, but as it happens, they make some of the best barbecue in Murfreesboro, a college town that happens to be the fastest-growing metropolitan area in the state. Owner Gary McGuire says he worked in restaurants as a teenager and college student, even as he made a career as a teacher and writer of computer software. Now with his grown sons and a dedicated chef and manager, he has built a barbecue restaurant, microbrewery, and Irish pub all in one. And it's constantly packed.

They dry rub, smoke, and pull their pork and chicken, and it's terrific. The chicken is freshly pulled when you order. Unlike most barbecue joints in this book, I'm going to tell you right now to order the House Salad topped with pork barbecue—or chicken, if your tastes go that way, but I favor the pork. Go really out on a limb and have it with the house mango chardonnay vinaigrette. If that sounds hoity-toity for a barbecue place, just trust me. You'll start craving barbecue salads (I recently ate three of these in one week).

"We love to pull our barbecue in public," Gary says. "It's cooked to perfect tenderness, we just pull off the fat layer and it falls apart." Of course, they make their own rubs and tailor them to the proteins.

Of course, you can't ever go wrong ordering pork or chicken OPQ (as they call it) sandwich. Make sure you order with a pint of Gary's son Andrew's beer. They've generally got two different in-house options available, plus several others, local and otherwise, on tap.

Don't get me wrong, the Irish specialties are also worth a trip back, particularly the fish and chips, but this is one Irish pub you come to with barbecue on your mind. Closed Monday.

Peg Leg Porker

903 Gleaves St., Nashville, TN 37203; (615) 829-6023; peglegporker .com

Carey Bringle, born in Memphis and raised mostly in Nashville (with significant regular visits back west), learned to cook barbecue from his uncle, a guy who competed at the first-ever Memphis in May. He began competing on Memphis in May team with his cousins in the late 1980s: "We were quite the party crew, we got kicked out in '89." He reformed the group and came back in 1991 with Ernie Mellor and Tripp Murray as team captains. They took second in pork shoulder that year and went on to pull off two more second-place

finishes over the next decade. Ernie went on to cater with his company Hog Wild (hogwildbbq.com) in Memphis, and Tripp went on to work for Harrah's casino. Carey came home to Nashville, and Peg Leg Porker was born.

Bringle's vision is a Memphis-style place like his childhood favorites in Nashville—that means cinder-block walls; blues, not country playing in the background; and a million wonderful family pictures blown up on the walls— the story of Bringle family over the past 60-plus years and their ties to barbecue. He cooks (by which I mean hickory smokes) whole hog, as well as shoulders, butts, and ribs. "This is as close to what I grew up on as possible. We don't serve brisket. I wanted to build a place as near to what I went to as child as possible."

He's master of the dry rub (applied at the end, in place of sauce). Order the ribs on your first visit and a side of beans—baked or green, both superb. I happen to adore the smoked green beans (the recipe can be found at the back of this book, by the way). The macaroni and cheese is darned good. Also high on the must-try list are the barbecue nachos—made as they were originally intended to be—chips, cheese, pulled pork, sauce, jalapeños—no extras. Bringle

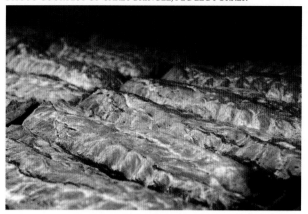

is very firm on that. And of course, you can never go wrong with a pork sandwich. (I love the ribs, though—*love* them.)

There's beer, but for the love of God, in Carey's place, order a bourbon cocktail or just straight bourbon. You'll find one of the best bourbon and whiskey bars in the area inside this barbecue joint, so don't miss the chance to partake of something really extraordinary. Among the most fun options is Peg Leg Porker's signature house bourbon, so make sure to give it a try.

This place is the best reason to fight the downtown traffic in the Gulch neighborhood I can think of.

Prater's

620 Woodbury Hwy., Manchester, TN 37355, (931) 954-5377; 9576 Manchester Hwy., Morrison, TN 37357, (931) 635-2259

I've never been to Prater's, I have to confess, but my friends who live in the area around McMinnville and Manchester absolutely swear by it. "It's really good 'cue," says Steve Corn of McMinnville. "Make sure you tell them that." The prices are fairly moderate as well. In an area where, honestly, most food is fast or from a chain of some kind, a local restaurant with good barbecue is kind of a godsend. It's also pretty warm and welcoming—and usually has peanuts on the tables for you to munch on while you wait for your plate of ribs.

In addition to their regular menu, they offer daily specials, but the regular menu gets constant raves. The pulled pork is really good—enough that you can just skip the sauce. Ditto on the ribs. You'll also find chicken, sandwiches (including burgers), barbecue nachos, and catfish. And the portions of both meats and sides are reputably sizable. On the side, the beans, both baked and white, get plenty of orders, as do French fries, coleslaw, and fried pickles (they've really gotten to be a Tennessee thing of late).

If you want to eat where the locals eat in this part of the state, Prater's is it. Sorry, no website or social media page yet, but you can find them at urbanspoon.com. There's also a location on SR 55 as you head between Manchester and McMinnville; it's small and right by the road and the perfect place to stop on that stretch because there's nothing to compare between McMinnville and I-24.

Puckett's Grocery and Restaurant

120 Fourth Ave. S., Franklin, TN 37064, (615) 794-5527; 500 Church St., Nashville, TN 37219, (615) 770-2772; 15 Public Sq., Columbia, TN, 38401, (931)490-4550; puckettsgrocery.com

Puckett's isn't strictly a barbecue restaurant, but when owner Andy Marshall opened his original grocery-café concept in Leiper's Fork outside Franklin in 1998, he quickly fell in love in with the barbecue cooking concept, and it has remained the most popular menu item by far at all locations over more than 15 years. And it's just good. Marshall is confident enough to say that he'd put it up against anyone else's, anywhere.

"There's a lot of good barbecue out there," says Marshall. "A lot of people around here don't look at it as an art, but as a revenue stream." For him, it's art. He began by buying a slow smoker, "borrowing" a winning rub from friends with a competitive barbecue team, and began his barbecuing career. He rubs his pork butts with the dry rub, slow cooks them for 9 straight hours and then wraps them in plastic and lets them sit for another nine, building up some fantastic flavor while maintaining moisture.

AMY WHIDBY

"It's a sous vide process, it sits in its own juices for hours," says Marshall. The process is consistent across all locations, so the quality is too. The barbecue chicken is really great as well. If you want it, go for the barbecue sliders.

Puckett's uses the meat-and-three concept, so you order with one, two, or three sides. The sweet potato fries and coleslaw must be considered strongly as two of three. The turnip greens are pretty darn good as well. Order dessert, and make sure it's pie or cobbler. If you go with a family member who just doesn't do barbecue, I suggest the "build your own burger" option to keep the family happy.

Puckett's has a good family atmosphere, with live music many evenings (the schedule is online). There's also a full bar for the over-21 crowd, with good beer, including some local microbrews, and a very solid cocktail selection. As with many larger Tennessee barbecue restaurants, a good selection of whiskey and bourbon goes without saying.

There are plenty of Puckett's locations. Marshall is a master of making his own tiny chain work and keeping it from feeling generic or chain-like. I tend to hang out near home in Franklin, but every location does things right. And they have their own food truck too—well, food trolley.

Rib City

780 West Jackson St., Cookeville, TN 38501; (931) 372-7100; ribcity .com; facebook.com/pages/Rib-City-Cookeville/314710419677

Rib City specializes in comfort foods, which is pretty much the hallmark of most southern-style restaurants, at least outside the big cities. If that's your aim, this place doesn't disappoint (and there are indeed a few franchises of Rib City across the country, with the original in Fort Myers, Florida). It's also one of the few places in its immediate area (on the border between Middle and East Tennessee) where you'll find a Carolina mustard–based sauce sharing table space with more classic mild and hot Tennessee styles.

The menu is actually large and diverse, but they clearly are smoking all their own meats, and barbecue is the dominant theme thereon. Barbecue pork and beef are good choices on the menu, although you'll likely be tempted by their burger options and even chicken and fish. There are also plenty of salads and a long list of sides, including sliced tomatoes, sweet potato fries, and garlic toast alongside slaw and potato salad.

Again, think comfort food when you walk in the door, and you have the right idea. There are lots of desserts on the menu. For dinner, there are sizable combo plates boasting options like shrimp and ribs, sirloins, and a full turkey and trimmings option.

Smoke Et Al

A NashvilleMobile Smokery and Catering; (615) 601-5993; smokeetal
.com

The whole food truck scene is s till rather new in the Nashville area, but among
the best things going on is Smoke Et Al. Owner Shane Autrey is a Memphis
native and professional chef who has worked under master chefs of the French
school and at very fine dining establishments across the region. He started his
career at 14 with a part-time dishwashing job and moved up and learned from
there, including from his grandmother and family cooks with abundant talent.
In Nashville, he worked for several years at the popular Mad Platter until his
wife challenged him to do it for himself and follow his barbecue passion, something he had built up in part thanks to participation in barbecue competitions
(he jokes about being pitmaster for a drinking team with a barbecue problem).

Autrey built on the concepts he had already developed for his competition
team, opening his mobile smoker in September 2011 and hitting the streets.
The truck (which he bought on Craigslist and revamped) works well for competition and catering as well, and
his team has done spectacularly
well at Memphis in May and the
Music City Barbecue Festival the
past few years.

All the dry rubs are made in-
house—as is practically everything
else. Autrey's philosophy is "feed
people," and the subhead is likely
"do it the way my MawMaw would
have done it."

The barbecue you get here is
labor intensive—all hardwood fired,
with shoulders cooking at least 12
hours. Among the must-tries are
the hot ribs, cut to single bones, dry
rubbed, smoked, fried, and tossed
in hot sauce—their version of Nashville's hot chicken. The Shoulder
Sammie Memphis Style is served
up with a vinegar slaw and crispy
bits of pork skin on a Kaiser roll, all
homemade.

On the side, don't miss the fried pickled okra—even if you don't like okra or fried pickles, give it a whirl: trust me. They do some great brisket tacos too. Most of the sides are vegetables with a bit (or a bunch) of smoke—this is one of the rare barbecue places where a vegetarian can order up the vegetables and feel perfectly safe. (Try the smoked apple and kale quesadilla.)

Rumor has it that a brick-and-mortar spot is forthcoming in the Wedgewood area of town. I sure hope so. Hours vary, so check the website.

Timberloft Barbecue and Catering

470 Gordonsville Hwy., Gordonsville, TN 38563; (615) 683-5070; timberloftrestaurant.com

I have to admit, the first couple of times I drove by Timberloft, I associated it with cool places like Bink's Outfitters in Murfreesboro, which sells Patagonia fleeces and outdoor gear, because of the name. I couldn't have been more wrong. Timberloft makes some mighty fine brisket, in their own words. It's also located right off I-40 between Lebanon and Cookeville, making it easy to find when you're looking to stop for lunch or dinner. If you're lucky, there's a trivia contest or a live performance going on while you're dining.

Timberloft makes for a pleasant dining experience, the decor is not unlike a nicer chain restaurant, and the atmosphere is warm. There is absolutely a bar in this one, with domestic and imported beer (including a few locals), artisan cocktails (try the apple Fireball martini, different and fun), and a wine list.

The menu is full of hickory-smoked options, a little bit Texas, a little bit Tennessee in style, though their take is billed as largely Texan. I'd start out with the Campfire Barbecue Nachos if you want something heavy; otherwise, go for the smoked wings. On the regular menu, the St. Louis–cut ribs are Memphis style, though the menu entry is a little confusing—dry rubbed and very good. Try ordering hickory-smoked pulled pork or Texas brisket sandwiches (depending whether you want to feel like you're in Nashville or Austin) or perhaps the barbecued chicken. For those who prefer a nonbarbecue option for dinner, there are steaks, burgers, and classic sandwiches, like the Reuben. There's a whole mac and cheese–themed series of dishes as well, including topping it with pork barbecue.

Prices are moderate but still a bit higher than you'll find at a roadside joint. To-go bulk orders are available, but this is also very much intended as a nicer, eat-in kind of place. Catering is available. Closed Monday.

Top Hog BBQ

642 Blythe Ave., Gallatin, TN; (615) 478-9330

Gallatin residents seem to regard Top Hog as one of their local secrets, but we Nashvillians in the know stop there when we're up on business. The white cinder-block building with a wide deck filled with outdoor seating makes for a terrific casual lunch or dinner. The barbecue style is very northern/Middle Tennessee traditional (again, when you see hoecakes on the menu with your barbecue, you pretty much know just where you are).

Look for pulled pork barbecue, smoked chicken, and baby back ribs on the menu (St. Louis cut, by the way). You'll also find catfish here, and it's easily a top seller. For those who want to go that way, burgers, grilled cheese, or a BLT can also be had. Also on the menu is fruit tea, which is something you almost always get in Middle Tennessee in the more genteel locales. Here, it's served up in a mason jar—at a guess, a blend of tea, lemonade, and orange juice—and never too sweet. Fruit tea is kind of our alternative to overly sweet teas. Coffee and soft drinks are also available.

On the side, I hear lots of praise for the deviled eggs, but the country fries, turnip greens, mac and cheese, or an order of white beans and corn bread don't sit badly on anyone, especially the last—for heaven's sake, while you're in this part of Tennessee, try some beans and corn bread.

Take home pulled pork by the pound and side items by the pint.

True's Barbeque

7837 Tennessee 25, Cross Plains, TN 37049; (615) 654-2838; trues barbeque.com

Cross Plains, where my master brewer friend Karen Lassiter and her husband Jack live, is for most people a stop on I-65 almost at the Tennessee–Kentucky border. Plenty of people hoping to get a good meal stop as they travel, however, for the taste of family-owned True's.

This is not a restaurant where there are 10 varieties of meat—you get pork or beef, generally—and that's okay because you'll enjoy it. If you don't want barbecue, grab a burger or some chicken strips, but really, you want the barbecue. Like many places in this stretch of what's still called Middle Tennessee, you'll find white beans cooked with onions on the menu as a side and also corn bread on which to consume your barbecue (hoecakes, in this case). If you aren't someone who has those constantly, choose them as your options.

Other Places to Visit

Both north and south of Nashville, there are a few places with good word of mouth you want to take a closer look at. Here are a few worth note.

Blue Smoke BBQ, 365 W. Bockman Way, Sparta, TN 38583; (931) 808-3280; facebook.com/pages/Blue-Smoke-Bbq/227012313977882
Closed Sunday.

Brickhouse Barbeque, 915 Nashville Hwy., Columbia, TN 38401-2432; (931) 490-0406
A cute little brick shop with tremendously good pork sandwiches, worth the stop.

JJ's Barbecue, 900 Hatcher Ln., Columbia, TN 38491; (931) 381-3463
Great hickory-smoked ribs, as well as pulled pork, turkey, and beef. Don't missed the stuffed baked potatoes.

Piggy's Place Bar-B-Que, 112 N. Anderson St., Tullahoma, TN 37388; (931) 455-5674
Piggy's bills itself as Mississippi wet-style barbecue, which in our vernacular means it's a little closer to Memphis than Middle Tennessee in its approach; the food is darned good. The ribs especially get a thumbs-up from guests.

Uncle Sonny's Bar B Que, 1505 N. Main St., Shelbyville, TN 37160; (931) 684-9010
A lot of my friends swear by this place. Both the pork and the brisket have a great reputation, and the fried pies are out of this world.

World Famous Jack of Hearts BBQ, 5075 Columbia Pike, Spring Hill, TN 37174; (931) 451-7887
Locally owned, for more than 10 years Jack of Hearts has been a must-visit in Spring Hill, just south of Franklin. Ribs, barbecue nachos, and outstanding house-made sauces make this a good place to try. A live music venue.

The homemade chili is a nice option, and there's a fried bologna sandwich on the menu to balance the usual hot dogs and such. Tuna, chicken, and egg salad sandwiches are there too, and that's old-fashioned Tennessee tradition itself—and what you expect mom or grandma to choose. And there's pizza, which is kind of a surprise but always works for kids especially. Homemade chess pie, peach cobbler, and chocolate fudge pie need to be ordered.

Takeout family packs and catering are available.

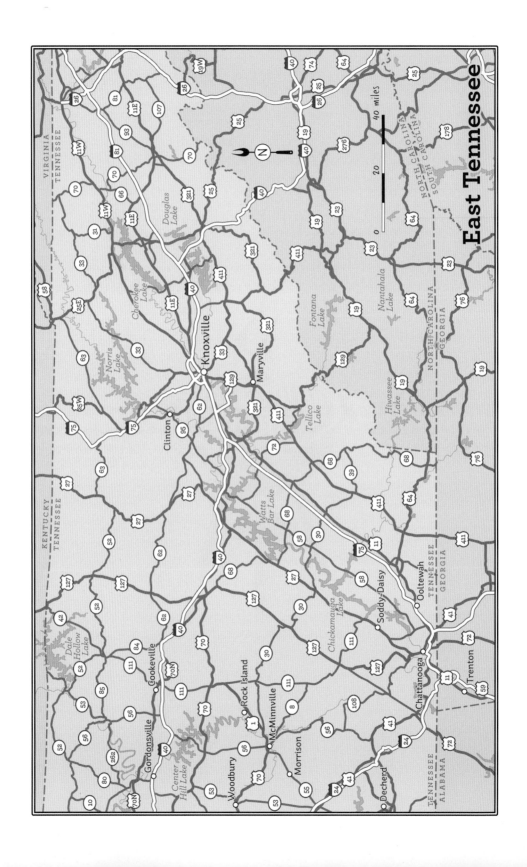

East Tennessee

East Tennessee

Stretching from Bristol on the Virginia border down to Knoxville and south-west to Chattanooga along I-75, East Tennessee is stunningly beautiful country. It's still mountainous, covered in forests and hollows. But it also plays home to a collection of impressive universities and colleges and myriad businesses. East Tennessee is its own place, much like the corners of western Virginia and North Carolina it touches. For years my family drove this stretch going "home" to see my late grandparents in Rocky Mount, Virginia. Somehow, we seemed to skip barbecue across this region and pick it up again in western Virginia. Man, were we wrong.

As I write this, my husband and his buddies are in Knoxville visiting our friends Vinnie and Kathy. They've gone to lunch at Dead End and are texting me pictures to taunt me (at home, writing). My cool friend TJ Vestal is in Chattanooga hitting Thatcher's for lunch. Barbecue is so part of the culture in Tennessee that it's almost taken for granted, but if I check social media on any given day, as many friends on this side of the world are hitting barbecue joints as in Memphis, Nashville, or Birmingham. And that tells me there's plenty going on.

East Tennessee is a gateway of sorts, the portal between Carolina style and Tennessee/Memphis style. In East Tennessee, you're likely to find sauces that are slightly thinner—more of a compromise between the thick sweetness of Memphis and the tarter vinegar tastes of Carolina. You're also more likely to find a mustard-based, South Carolina–type sauce. (Which, by the way, I love, and I don't care if that makes me a heathen. Of course, you also find a grand mustard sauce down at Big Bob Gibson's in Alabama.)

When you come out here, there are a few treks off the beaten path you must make. One is to Ridgewood Barbecue, way up near the Tennessee–Virginia border, where they're still smoking just hams the way they have been for decades. Owner Larry Profitt still runs the restaurant his parents began, and he'll pass it on to his own daughter in future.

I'm partial to George Ewart's Dead End in Knoxville, I have to admit, and when in Chattanooga, Sugar's Ribs can pull me right off the interstate. But there is so much good barbecue here, and, as with all the state, there are still little finds on the edges of the back roads. Thatcher's, outside Chattanooga, is one of those—technically, it's Georgia, but I'm okay with that. Like this whole region, we share cooking traditions.

Some of the restaurant owners will tell you that they learned everything from parents and local tradition; others, perhaps more than any other part of the state, will confess that they owe as much to the influence of Carolina—and sometimes Texas or Kansas City—as they do to Tennessee. And for this last part, you see that in the number of restaurants out here that serve beef brisket, for example.

But when it comes down to it, East Tennessee still owes as much to the same old-time traditions of cooking hogs that the rest of the state does. If they allow an influx of outside influences, if we're honest, Memphis ribs owe a little bit to St. Louis and Kansas City too, and Nashville has taken all of it and dared anyone to challenge its place as a Tennessee barbecue capital even so.

East Tennessee produces some fine barbecue, and it's our tradition, even if they wink a little at a Carolina sauce now and then.

What follow are a few of my favorite East Tennessee locales, but as with all the other regions, remember to stop at the holes in the wall when you have the chance.

Archer's Barbecue

5415 Kingston Pike, Knoxville, TN 37919, (865) 394-9580; 7650 Oak Ridge Pkwy., 37931, (865) 281-3057; 6714 Central Avenue Pike, 37912, (865) 687-2694; archersbbq.com

Archer's Barbecue owner Archer Bagley is a native of Memphis, and he has brought his Memphis know-how to Knoxville. The popular barbecue restaurant now has three locations across the city—evidence it's become a true local favorite. Everything is made in-house in Bagley's own take on Memphis style. The interiors are crisp and contemporary, open and inviting. The food is fresh and delicious, the meats juicy and tender. (And among their chef crew is former *Dukes of Hazzard* actor Clark Cowan, who can cook up a storm.)

The menu is a solid mix of smoked meats—pork, chicken, brisket, and ribs, along with Angus franks. This is the kind of place you expect to be able to order a beer, and fortunately it is indeed available, both domestic and imported.

On the side, look for excellent collard greens, plus barbecue beans, creamed corn, and yummy sweet potato chips.

The sauces reflect the fact that they're in East Tennessee—you find a mild and a Memphis style, plus a spicy St. Louis, a sweet-hot Kansas City version, a really nice and spicy moonshine sauce, and a Carolina mustard style. And of course, it's available in large sizes to go for your own home projects of for catering and takeout accompaniment.

Bone's Smokehouse

9012 E. Brainerd Rd., Chattanooga, TN 37421; (423) 894-2663; facebook.com/BonesChattanooga?rf=116169535138428

The Hennen brothers opened Bone's in 1999, and it has maintained its place in the East Tennessee barbecue firmament. Look for pork, chicken, beef, turkey, and ribs on the menu, all prepared in hickory wood–fired smokers. Then the menu gets diverse in all kinds of unexpected ways, and that makes it fun.

Start out your meal with some of the Brunswick stew, which makes use of smoked chicken, beef, and pork all in a tomato base, or go off the traditional grid a bit for some barbecue quesadillas. The starters pretty fearlessly add barbecue to every possible popular food, including pizza, with very positive results. The fried pickles are a customer favorite.

Chicken dishes really shine here; you can get half a smoked chicken if you like, or try the smoked chicken pot pie or chicken enchiladas—again, the strength of this menu is in the creative ways it uses smoked meats effectively in foods we think we already know. The pulled pork plate and the ribs are still pleasers for the folks who came out for mainstream barbecue, never fear. A vegetable plate and vegetable lasagna appeal well to non–meat eaters who find they have stumbled into a vortex of smoked meats.

There is indeed a beer list—the usual suspects but a guarantee of a cold one to clear your throat—and also soft drinks and tea, as well as true root beer float for those craving sweet. The dessert menu offers a homemade cobbler of the day, carrot cake, and hot fudge cake.

The catering menu offers both barbecue and nonbarbecue items and holiday smoked turkey and ham for office or family needs. Closed Sunday.

Dead End BBQ

3621 Sutherland Ave., Knoxville, TN 37919, (865) 212-5655; 527 W. Broadway Ave., Maryville, TN 37801, (865) 240-2600; deadendbbq.com

Definitely a must-visit in this part of the state, Dead End has two locations to make that easier for you. George Ewart of Knoxville's Dead End says his grandmother used to make barbecue, and he still has her sauce recipe written on a recipe card. He started cooking with his dad out back in a pit when he was 14. When he moved to the Forest Heights neighborhood in 2000, he and a few neighbors roasted a hog on Memorial Day to encourage the neighbors to get

out and socialize, and one thing led to another. They started competing locally, then nationally, and winning, and by 2009 he was ready to open a restaurant with the help of a longtime friend.

Ewart takes pride in his chicken and brisket, believing them the toughest things to cook, but he has excellent pork and ribs as well. Smoked meats are big in the immediate area, and Ewart, from West Virginia originally, knows how to smoke some bologna with the best of them—and smoked sausage as well. Dead End is the only restaurant in the area doing brisket daily, and they introduced it to this side of the state.

Dead End makes its rubs particular to each variety of protein, and the flavors are better because of it. The sauces are excellent—if you like hot, make sure you try the Gratefully Dead. Dead End Red is a traditional tomato-based sauce, and Peacefully Dead handles the milder crowd.

Order the Competition Chicken or the Brisket on your first visit after starting with the smoked sausage and cheese, served with pita and beer mustard. The hot wings make a good starter as well. There's homemade banana pudding for dessert. The menu showcases a number of specialty sandwiches as well, but the barbecue purist will be happy going with the traditional offerings. My Knoxville friends swear by this place and do so for very good reason. Oh—get the sweet potato waffle fries.

Catering can be had, and so can barbecue classes for those who want the real experience. Sauces and rubs can also be ordered online. And if you want barbecue at your East Tennessee wedding, call Dead End.

Hickory Pit Bar-B-Que

5611 Ringgold Rd., Chattanooga, TN 37412; (423) 894-1217; hickory
pitbarbeque.com

Inside this cute little wooden building, there isn't a whole lot of seating room
in the neat and cozy interior, though there is a porch suitable for dining on
sunny days. That doesn't mean you shouldn't make the effort to get there. A
drive-through makes for ready pickup if the interior is packed at the lunch
hour. Inside, the restaurant shows its chops with a very thorough menu with
something to please most palates—perhaps that's why it has been operating
successfully since 1984.

The appetizers showcase all that lovers of the fiendishly delicious deep-
fried could want, from chicken to fried mushrooms and pickles. Jalapeño pop-
pers get their own place on the menu, as do some intriguing-sounding "dino
bites"—deep fried broccoli and cheddar. Those will get anyone to eat broccoli,
believe me.

The barbecue itself is hickory smoked with a dry rub, then sauced with the
restaurant's signature sauce. Look for pork, beef, and chicken and pork ribs,
and, if you're so inclined, there's chopped Black Angus steak and big barbecue
stuffed potatoes. On the weekend, fried catfish makes the Saturday specials
list. You can get your kid a corn dog for $1.50, which, combined with a few tater
tots, should make the young ones happy as can be. On the more grown-up
side, a smoked chicken salad sandwich, BLT, and even fried bologna sandwich
allows for some mixing up of your usual barbecue joint favorites.

For dessert lovers, apple pie, cheesecake, and funnel cake join the banana
pudding to make sure that you'll want to finish up with something sweet. Tea
and soft drinks served; no bar.

Hillbilly Willy's Barbecue and Catering Company

115A Browns Ferry Rd., Chattanooga, TN 37419, (423) 821-2272; 9203
Lee Hwy., Ooltewah, TN 37363, (423) 602-8644; hillbillywillys.com

Hillbilly Willy's easily ranks as one of Chattanooga's most popular barbecue spots, though the menu is fairly expansive. If your taste runs to more
traditional sit-down restaurant fare, you can find it here, along with plenty
of good barbecue that's distinctly reminiscent of Memphis (though owner
George Foster says he developed his own methods). The Ooltewah location
predates Chattanooga, but it seems like the Chattanooga location gets the
publicity. Either choice should please, especially given the moderate cost of
your meal.

East Tennessee Travel

When you're traveling in East Tennessee, the **Smoky Mountains** and the areas around Pigeon Forge, with its super popular **Dollywood,** come to mind. That's not a bad thing, but there are plenty of additional trips worth making. I highly recommend a stay in Chattanooga, which has enough attractions to make its own travel book.

Chattanooga Bluff View Arts District (bluffviewartdistrict.com)—Shops, artisan workshops, walking and biking trails that lead along the river—there's a whole day's exploration to be done in Chattanooga's beautiful arts district. Visit bakeries, drink wine, sample chocolate, and take the time to see all the fantastic art.

Dollywood Amusement Park and Pigeon Forge (dollywood.com)—When Dolly Parton does something big, she does it right. This Smoky Mountain amusement park will thrill kids of all ages and keep them coming back. Whether your thing is games, shows, or roller coasters, it's got it. Nearby in Pigeon Forge, there are plenty of other attractions, like the Titanic Museum (really—and it's wonderful) to keep you entertained for a long weekend, and the prices are reasonable for a multiday stay.

Gatlinburg (gatlinburg.com)—Whether you want to try skiing in the South (this is one of our few local ski resorts) or enjoy the mountains at the heart of summer, Gatlinburg is a little less touristy than popular Pigeon Forge but full of fun things to do. There are two relatively new moonshine distilleries (Ol' Smoky and Davy Crockett), plenty of good restaurants, and an abundance of incredible views over the mountains. This is a lovely place to stay the weekend. In the right weather, they even have a little ski resort.

Lookout Mountain/Ruby Falls/Rock City (seerockcity.com, lookoutmountain.com, rubyfalls.com)—Rock City may be the granddaddy of tourist attractions, but it remains a fun stop in its own right. I love Ruby Falls, which offers a walk a mile deep into the mountain to see a spectacular waterfall that really is

(continued)

everything promised by those roadside signs. Lookout Mountain, meanwhile, offers some of the most breathtaking views in the state. For once, take a risk and stop—all those signs on barns can't be wrong.

Tennessee Aquarium at Chattanooga (tnaqua.org)—One of the very best aquariums in the Southeast, this is a must-visit if you have kids (though it's pretty fun for grown-ups as well). The penguins alone will capture your attention and keep you laughing, and the jellyfish exhibit makes for a lot of "oohs" and "aahhs." Me, I love the river otters. Even for locals, this is a regular visit to see what's new, at least a couple of times a year. The 3D IMAX theater always has a great nature show going.

The regular menu is full of the barbecue standards, ranging from pork, beef, and chicken sandwiches to slabs of ribs. There are burgers for those who really crave a cheeseburger. The daily specials expand into the above-mentioned sit-down realm—steaks, pasta, pork loin, and pot roast all have their days. The barbecue fries loaded with meat looked like a fun alternative to the loaded barbecue potatoes (which Hillbilly Willy's also offers). The sides, including barbecue beans, fire-roasted corn, and fresh collards, as well as the usual potato salad and coleslaw, all stack up. Fans of barbecue salads will also be able to indulge here, getting their veggies while enjoying smoked meats at the same time.

The made-from-scratch daily desserts include Coca-Cola Cake (something you need to try at least once in the South), Derby Pie (a variation on classic pecan), and ubiquitous but still wonderful banana pudding.

Of course, "party pack" and barbecue by the pound are available to go. A full catering menu can be found on the website. Closed Sunday.

Porker's Bar-B-Cue

1251 Market St., Chattanooga, TN 37402; (423) 267-2726; porkersbbq
.com

Porker's is a Chattanooga favorite downtown, known for its kitschy decor, showcasing a big Elvis painting, Coca-Cola memorabilia, and more. Founded by local barbecue aficionado Clarke Cook in the late 1980s, he passed it on to Lawrence and Diana Mills, whom he trained, and they in turn to their nephew and his wife, Beau and Tracy Tucker, who own and operate the place today. Over the years, they've played host to plenty of celebrities as well as the local and tourist crowds and have even fed former President George W. Bush.

There's a diverse menu to appeal to everyone at Porker's, which remains a beloved local staple even after more than 20 years. You'll find the classics—smoked pork, beef, chicken, turkey, ham, and ribs, plus smoked meatloaf for something rather different but delicious. They recommend trying the grilled marinated chicken sandwich, but visitors rave about the traditional smoked pork and chicken.

You won't find corn bread on this menu, but you will get the option of Texas toast or rolls, as well as the usual bun. There's a deep list of side items, and the coleslaw and potato salad pair very well with a barbecue sandwich. Don't look for a bar in this family restaurant, but there are plenty of soft-drink choices and definitely milk shakes—yum.

Desserts are plentiful, so definitely save room. The Oreo Cookie pie and Key lime pie might be worth coming in for on their own. Closed Saturday and Sunday.

Ridgewood Barbecue

900 Elizabethton Hwy., Bluff City, TN 37618; (423) 538-7543; facebook
.com/pages/Ridgewood-Barbecue/111550848884507

Larry Proffitt's parents started Ridgewood in 1948, and the restaurant has been around ever since. These days, it's Larry and his daughter, Lisa Proffitt Peters, who keep things running smoothly and commit to maintaining the restaurant's philosophy and its food quality. "I strive to keep the same product my mother and father developed," he says. "I aim for consistency, and barbecue is labor intensive."

The short version is this: Make the detour off the highway and go eat lunch here. Seriously.

Ridgewood is known for a very particular style of barbecue. When the Proffitt family cooks, it's hams—not shoulders like most of the major barbecue joints in this part of the country. They're smoked over hickory wood, making

for a fantastic sliced, smoked pork sandwich. The smoky sauce is a secret recipe passed down to Larry from his mother, and only the family knows it.

"Barbecue to me has a connotation of fire and smoke," says Proffitt. "So I make sure it's smoked with hickory.

Everything is made to the same exacting, from-scratch specifications daily—the cabbages turn into slaw, the Idaho peelers turn into gorgeous French fries. The smoked barbecue beans are definitely on the must-try list. And when you're placing your order, don't forget a side of the house blue cheese dressing with a few little packets of crackers. The extra-thick dressing is to die for, according to local fans and tourists alike. Made from another secret family recipe, folks order it with small packets of crackers to dip and rave about the ridiculously delicious flavor. Closed Sunday.

Riverview Grill

1625 Oak Ridge Hwy., Clinton, TN 33716; (865) 463-8550; riverview grill.com

Houssein and Jill Ghodrat took over the space that became their popular Clinton barbecue restaurant in January 2011. Prior to that, they had a place in downtown Knoxville, but when they lost the lease, they decided to start over in a new area, with a new style—barbecue and seafood. Houssein said he didn't have abundant experience with barbecue prior to finding the space, but it had a smoker, so he painstakingly taught himself—now his barbecue wins

awards around East Tennessee. It's very much East Tennessee style, with three sauces—house, sweet, and spicy—none of which are heavily based in vinegar.

The pork barbecue and the delicious fried catfish sell with equal vigor, and making a second trip for seafood or doing a barbecue-and-seafood combo is recommended. If you come in with a friend, check out the Smokehouse Barbecue Combo for Two, with pork, brisket, ribs, and a half chicken. Houssein Ghodrat says a visiting Memphis in May judge once came back to the kitchen and sang the praises of this particular option, and that's pretty easy to believe. (Ghodrat adds that he has never eaten Memphis barbecue.)

You'll find all the traditional meats here, including two types of chicken— both chopped and whole quarters. Try the quarters; they're incredibly popular with the locals. On the side, order coleslaw, barbecue beans, and potato salad. Save room for dessert, especially the super-rich peanut butter pie—so rich you may want to split it with a friend.

There are three beers on tap—generally Yuengling, Miller Lite, and Bud Lite—and plenty more by the bottle.

Catering is available. There's also a good kid's specialty menu for your picky eaters who want chicken tenders or peanut butter and jelly. It's a great family experience.

"Our portions are huge," says Ghodrat. "Come by, we'll feed you until you can't move." That sounds great—as long as you save enough room for that pie.

The Chains:
Sonny's Real Pit Bar-B-Que

The Sonny's franchise remains popular across this part of the South—the only Tennessee location is currently in Knoxville, but they proliferate in North Georgia, with a few in Kentucky and Alabama. The chain was started by Floyd Tillman (a.k.a. "Sonny") in Gainesville, Florida, and franchised over the years. Tillman sold the company to some of his franchise holders, Jeff and Bob Yarmuth, in the early 1990s.

The Knoxville franchise (350 N. Peters Rd.) remains popular with residents. The company smokes meat over oak rather than hickory—which gives it a distinctly different taste, if you happen to be a connoisseur of that sort of thing. You'll get smoked pork, beef, chicken, and turkey (sampler platters allow you to try multiple options, and most meats can be gotten either pulled or sliced) and the usual cadre of barbecue sides, including coleslaw and mac and cheese. The smoked chicken wings and fried okra make solid choices as starters, as do the onion rings.

On the nonbarbecue side, find plenty of salad, a hearty steak burger, grilled chicken sandwiches, and fried shrimp. There's a Double Chocolate Brownie Bliss dessert option that should keep one's sweet tooth content.

Sonny's style seems to blend a little Tennessee, a little Texas, and a touch of Kansas City, but you expect that sort of hybrid in a lot of chain restaurants founded outside a particular barbecue region.

Shuford's Smokehouse Barbecue and Catering

924 Signal Mountain Rd., Chattanooga, TN 37405, (423) 267-0080;
11320 Dayton Pike, Soddy-Daisy, TN 37379, (423) 451-7102; shufords
bbq.com

Shuford's is a real true hole-in-the-wall joint, set in a refurbished old gas station along Signal Mountain (with a second small location now in Soddy-Daisy). It doesn't have a pretentious rafter in its entire restaurant, but it does have great food, and it's all pretty much in the traditional barbecue genre.

Inside, the decor is heavy on SEC football (hope you like Tennessee or Alabama) and plain tables and chairs. If they have a legend after 20 years in business, it's probably their sauces, made right there by owner Jeff Davis and kept secret from everyone. There's a sweet option and a hot option—I'll take the hot every time, but it's not made for the faint of palate.

(Note: The smaller, second location falls into the barbecue stand category and currently has limited hours, just Wednesday through Saturday, 11 a.m. to 8 p.m., but that could change.)

On the menu, in addition to the usual pork, chicken, beef, turkey, and ribs, add options like Polish sausage and ham. Brunswick stew, turkey legs, and chili fill out the specialties list—although really on a first visit, go with a sandwich, then diversify as you return.

The coleslaw is darned good. Family packs go out the door at great prices, and you can order custom smoked meats, have events catered, and even order up a small smoked young pig in advance for a party or family gathering.

Barbecue-joint staple banana pudding is readily available, if you still have room after you eat your meal. Soft drinks, tea, and lemonade are complemented by the availability of beer. Drive-through service is helpful, and the service across the board impresses. One thing you'll notice is that customers seem to be largely regulars, and they come back frequently. That's a very good sign.

Sugar's Ribs

2450 15th Ave., Chattanooga, TN 37404, (423) 826-1199; 507 Broad St., Chattanooga, TN 37402, (423) 508-8956; sugarsribscom

Sugar's Ribs prides itself in being the kind of barbecue place you find off the beaten path, but it conveniently has two locations—one in downtown Chattanooga and one right off the highway on I-24 as you're driving through. Owners Lawton and Karen Haygood also own a couple of more traditional restaurants, including the extremely good Boathouse Rotisserie and Raw Bar, but it's Sugar's that draws in the major tourist and traveling crowds. While I

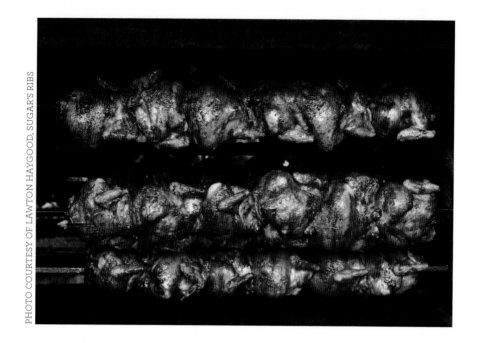

first discovered it on a food journalist press trip, it has become a standby while driving to visit my husband's relatives in Atlanta from the Nashville area.

Lawton says that when he got into the barbecue business, he quickly discovered how hard it was to make truly good barbecue, cooking all night to have it ready for the next day and trying to keep it at its absolute best flavor for the customer. "We're about the flavor of the meat," he says. "I don't like the too heavy smoke you get with Texas barbecue, and I'm not a fan of a heavy dry rub the way you get with some West Tennessee stuff."

Because of its location off the interstate, about 65 percent of the 15th Avenue location's business is travelers, but surveys tell the Haygoods that many are repeat customers. That's not a surprise—the ribs are excellent, and so is the pork barbecue. Unlike many southern Tennessee locations, barbecued lamb is on the menu, and it's quite good.

There's a wide selection of side items, the classics, and some Texas-style options, like chili and fire-roasted jalapeños. The Reese's and Hershey's pies deserve some dessert-time attention.

Choose from five table sauces, ranging from sweet to hot, depending on your taste, but know that the flavor of the meat here is good enough that you can do without if you choose. Beer is in bottles and on draft, and wine is by the glass. The downtown location, heavily frequented by business travelers, has a very extensive double bar, featuring fine bourbons and tequilas.

Sweet P's Barbecue and Soul House

3725 Maryville Pike, Knoxville, TN 37920; (865) 247-7748; sweetpbbq
.com

Chris Ford's first career was rock and roll, and as a musician, he toured the
nation, especially the South, exploring every little mom-and-pop restaurant
and barbecue joint he could. "I fell in love with barbecue," he says. When he
came to the end of his music career, he settled in the Knoxville area with his
wife and child and spent serious time perfecting his barbecue skills (at the
time, good local barbecue was pretty rare) and catering while he learned the
business. The restaurant came about when he found a "shack" by the river.
The owner had trouble keeping tenants and offered it to him rent free. He
partnered with a cousin with solid restaurant business knowledge and leapt
into the restaurant world.

"I just wanted to cook and have some really good sides, fresh and modern,
things that appealed to the community," says Ford. He makes use of two local
farmers to supply him where he can, and he also makes sure there are side
items and vegetables suitable for his vegetarian customers.

"I try to keep the meat old school and simple—use a great rub, sweat it for
a day, then cook slow and low over a mix of hickory wood and white oak. We're
pretty heavy on the smoky flavor," he says.

Ford defines his sauces as "East Tennessee"—a compromise between
the vinegar of North Carolina and the sweeter, heavier Memphis style. Your
options are "thin" sauce, a vinegar and tomato blend; "thick," tomato based

Other East Tennessee Options

With their blend of styles, East Tennessee is a fun place to explore the barbecue options. Don't go into any expecting a pure experience, either Tennessee or Carolina. There are many good places to try out this way, but here are some diverse options that might be helpful if you're making a drive through the Smoky's particularly.

Chandler's Deli, 3101 E. Magnolia Ave., Knoxville, TN 37914; (865) 595-0212
A little more meat-and-three style than strictly a barbecue joint, though the owners clearly love barbecue. One of the few places around with chitterlings and chicken livers on the regular menu, as well as good ribs, both beef and pork. Look for many side options (that meat-and-three thing) and a crazy selection of good desserts.

Hungry Bear BBQ, 2263 East Pkwy., Gatlinburg, TN, (865)325-8048; 490 East Pkwy., Gatlinburg, TN 37738, (865) 325-1084
There are a few locally owned barbecue spots up in the Gatlinburg area, and Hungry Bear is one of the most popular. Good classic pulled pork and sides.

M&M Catering, 1039 Summer Wood Rd., Knoxville, TN 37923; (865) 692-1003
They call themselves catering, but they've got plenty of carryout as well, with relatively short hours (about 11 a.m. to 7 p.m. daily). Pork, beef and chicken quarters, traditional sides, and some truly spectacular desserts; a good option if you've got an event or party to provide for.

Rickard Ridge BBQ, 131 Goose Ln., Caryville, TN 37714; (423) 907-8202
They claim they're worth the drive into the Smoky's and, quite frankly, make a nice alternative to the Pigeon Forge collection of chain places. The breaded pickles rock, so start with those and move on to pulled pork, ribs, or some excellent smoked chicken thighs.

but not overly sweet; and "hot," which combines the thin sauce with a chipotle pepper puree.

The ribs are a must-try here, as is the BBQ burrito, with chicken or pork, beans, slaw, cheese, and sauce wrapped in a tortilla (you might have seen it on *Man vs. Food*). On the side, try the mac and cheese, or else get a Tomato N' Blues Salad with chopped tomatoes, cucumbers, and yellow peppers tossed with chunks of blue cheese and homemade tomato vinaigrette.

Just about the only thing not made in-house is the dessert, which come from Magpie's—a brilliant Knoxville bakery worth a stop itself. You'll also find plenty of southern regional beers to go with your lunch or dinner.

Live music happens about twice monthly, ranging from singer/songwriter nights to blues.

Thatcher's Barbecue & Grille

35 Price St., Trenton, GA 30752, (706) 657-6465; 1214 US 41 N., Calhoun, GA 30701; (706) 625-6465; thatchersbbq.com

"We're just everyday people working hard to please," says owner John Thatcher modestly of the two barbecue restaurants he and wife, Melanie, own in the Chattanooga area. For the two of them, it has been a labor of love, and they're still committed to using their own recipes and smoking meat the old-fashioned way in stick burner smokers with hickory wood. While they are technically in Georgia, both locations are in the immediate Chattanooga area—Trenton, off I-75 South at exit 318, and Calhoun, off I-59 at exit 11 (both just off I-24 through Tennessee).

As I spoke to John, he was putting 32 pork butts on to smoke—a labor of love for him daily. It goes without saying that Thatcher's has built its reputation on pork, but they're very proud of the brisket there as well. You can top your meats with one of three sauces—a sweet, a hot, and a spicy—or a "Carolina gold" mustard–based option. The ribs and chicken also have a following.

High on the most popular list is the pork plate with two sides—get the potato salad (from Melanie's own recipe) and Melanie's mac and cheese (available only for dinner). Recommended is the Cowboy Spud, topped with pulled pork, and its sister, the Cowgirl Spud, topped with barbecue chicken.

Desserts are pudding-centric—aim for the peanut butter banana pudding or the strawberry shortcake pudding. You'll have no cause for regret, except perhaps a few calories.

The Trenton location offers both indoor and outdoor seating; the Calhoun location is indoor only. Expect a wait on Saturdays. Thatcher's is a quiet gem of a barbecue joint—you'll feel like you've been let in on a big, wonderful secret. Closed Sunday.

The Outliers: North Alabama & Beyond Tennessee's Borders

Why on earth does what happens in North Alabama concern lovers of Tennessee barbecue? I would say because North Alabama has the same rich traditions and a lot of the same philosophies as Tennessee—perhaps even more so, even though no one talks about Alabama barbecue with the same kind of hushed tones reserved so strongly for Tennessee and for Memphis. They don't have a festival comparable to Memphis in May or Jack Daniel's, it's true. But there's something real and important going on here all the same. To deny it—or to deny its ties with the same kind of deep traditions as Tennessee—is to miss something very important.

The Alabama taste and style shares more in common with Tennessee than it does with North Carolina or any other tradition. When I talked with Jim Myers during his tenure at the Fatback Project early on in the process of writing this book, one of the first things he said to me was that he felt that Alabama, almost more than Tennessee, was a focal point for the same kind of serious pit smoking tradition as its northern neighbor. That may not gel in everyone's minds, but it does underline the reality that while we try to compartmentalize barbecue, it's rarely as easy to pinpoint what came from where as we'd like to think. Alabama and Tennessee have a huge amount in common.

If you want to see what has helped impact the growth of Tennessee barbecue over the years, look at what's going on in Birmingham, with Jim N' Nick's, Saw's, and Dreamland, and in Decatur, with Big Bob Gibson's (at the 2014 Jack Daniel's Invitational, the Big Bob's team took fourth place overall and won the sauce category hands down—again).

There's also no arguing that Jim Pihakis of Jim N' Nick's has become the godfather of all regional barbecue, from his now nearly 30-year-old restaurant chain to his creation of the Fatback Pig Project to his support of farmers and traditional southern foodways. There was some discussion of his impact in the Middle Tennessee chapter, but this one should confirm why he also rightfully has a place among the outliers who impact Tennessee's long-term barbecue culture.

The Fatback Pig Project

You've probably never heard of Eva, Alabama, a small town a couple of hours down I-65 into North Alabama not too far from Cullman. But remember that name because something extraordinary and paradigm shifting is happening there: a hog processing plant.

That may not sound exciting, but the plant belongs to the Fatback Pig Project. At its not-to-distant inception, it was overseen by foodie extraordinaire Jim Myers, best known for his food activism and highly admirable career as a food critic in Nashville. He recently left Fatback and returned to work at *The Tennessean* newspaper, and the project is now managed by a board rather than an individual, according to founder Nick Pihakis. The group of writers and chefs who surround and support it include six Beard-nominated chefs and some fairly influential southern food personalities, including John T. Edge of Southern Foodways Alliance. The important part of all this—and the reason for the need to drop significant names like Jim and John T.—is that it aims to change the way we buy pork.

The story starts a bit like this: Nick Pihakis, founder of Jim N' Nick's, finds himself driving around Mississippi in a pickup truck with a farmer friend and in the course of the discussion realizes just how much hog farming, once a staple down here, has declined in the recent past. One of those reasons is the difficulty in finding hog processing with any consistent regularity in this part of the South.

The economics just don't seem to allow for processors remaining in business, and in turn the farmers don't see the point in raising animals they then have to transport vast distances, cutting swaths into their own profit margin. Unsurprisingly, many of them turn instead to raising crops like corn, which provide a much easier market these days and ready money.

Pihakis brings the issue up to a handful of chef friends, and an idea comes: What if they had their own processing plant, which was also a production facility—providing products like bacon and sausage and charcuterie, as well as regular cuts of meat? What if they focused not on commodity hogs but on heritage breeds, like Berkshire and Duroc, and those hogs were raised in a sustainable environment, without chemicals, hormones, and antibiotics?

ANGIE MOSIER

Nick Pihakis

In conjunction came the Fatback Collective, a related group. It began as a few of those fellows, including Nick, were musing over beer one night about the possibility of using a heritage breed of hog in a big-time competition, with a commitment to showing off the flavor and exploring cooking technique. They decided it was worth a try, and the Collective was born. A rookie team in 2011, they took home third at Memphis in May in the whole hog division—no small feat for a new team.

The confluence of these two moments led to the Fatback Pig Project—a paradigm shift in the world of southern hog raising and processing. It meant buying the above-mentioned plant and getting it operational. The group buying included Nick, Will Harris of White Oak Pastures, Rose Sarris and Anthony Anselmo of SRA Meats in Birmingham, Michael Bodnar, John Michael Bodnar, and Matt Bodnar.

The goal was manifold: First, they wanted to simply provide good pork, which didn't necessarily seem a viable option given the regional decline of small hog farming. To make that happen, they needed what Jim Myers calls "hooves on the ground"—to make that pork readily available by supporting existing and new small farmers who dedicate themselves to raising the heritage breeds sustainably across the region.

(continued)

ANGIE MOSIER

Heritage hogs, like the Berkshire, says Myers, are the equivalent of Angus beef or heirloom tomatoes. "They're old school, preindustrialized, pastured, and naturally fed." If that sounds like the direction you want to see your chefs moving, you're not alone.

They needed the processing facility to make sure they had "farrow-to-finish control," from breeding pigs that are good mothers and raising and feeding them well to making sure there's a short travel time to the slaughter and being certain their killing happens humanely. The results offer high-quality meat with good marbling (of the kind that's bred out of most commodity hogs these days). More, they needed it to be a USDA-certified facility where all aspects of every process are done by the book.

To make that worthwhile for the farmers, they absolutely required a solid market for those pigs as well, and that's found with the above-mentioned chefs and others like them who either buy in quantity or have a ready audience prepared to pay top dollar for the quality of the meat.

With the processing plant also comes product, so that Fatback can produce a plethora of specialized products both for their own branded sales and for specialty markets. Those include bacon and sausages under the Fatback Pig

Project name; custom-created breakfast sausage, Andouille, kielbasa, Tabasco bacon, and more for John Currance's Big Bad Breakfast in Oxford, Mississippi; specialty products for Chef Donald Links's Couchon Butcher in New Orleans and Links's sister project Germantown market in Nashville scheduled to open in Fall of 2015; and a wide range of additional specialty products only just being realized.

(Jim Myers departed in the fall 2014 after having spent his time with Fatback traveling weekly between Eva and his family in Nashville. Of him, Pihakis says, "Jim has done so many good things for us, we can never repay him for all that.")

Nick Pihakis says that as the business has gotten started, they've found it's actually quite difficult to compete in the raw pork market with the large-scale producers at the present time, but they've found early success with the value-added products they're creating. That now includes products made for companies like Inland Seafood, Carroll's Sausage, Whole Foods, and the bacon served at Jim N' Nick's restaurants.

"We're working hard on the retail side, looking at getting units into grocery stores," says Pihakis. He points out that many regional groceries tied to large-scale chains like Publix, Winn Dixie, and Piggly Wiggly have a fair amount of latitude in terms of bringing in and selling items specific to the local market. While he's currently in talks with several of those stores, he's also excited about the prospect of their new Birmingham fulfillment warehouse, which will allow anyone to visit the website (fatbackpig.com) and purchase their products.

The ultimate goal is not only to serve the more than 30 regional restaurants from Tennessee to Louisiana that have committed to using their products but also to build the market and supply more businesses, with a long-term eye toward producing enough that it influences prices for regular customers looking to buy pork to serve at home too. In other words, they're creating whole new infrastructure centered around producing something that changes the vision for pork production in the South. They're off to a good start with their value-added products readily available to customers online and at particular businesses. And of course, they are generating the hope that other regions will follow their lead.

To Find Fatback Products

Big Bad Breakfast
719 North Lamar, Oxford, MS 38655, (662) 236-2666; 5361 US 280, Birmingham, AL; citygroceryonline.com

Cochon Butcher
930 Tchoupitoulas St., New Orleans, LA 70130; (504) 588-7675; cochonbutcher.com

The Fatback Pig Project
130 Daniels Chapel Rd., Eva, AL 35621; (205) 451-1868; fatbackpig.com
Online market available
Additional information at jimnnicks.com

ANGIE MOSIER

Just as in Tennessee, when you drive the highways of Alabama, you'll find myriad little places with a smoker out back serving up some truly amazing barbecue. I make a lot of drives down I-65 into North Alabama. Occasionally, there's a stop at some little stand, like Johnny's in Cullman, and the end results are inevitably pleasing. It's problematic to try to document most of these places because some disappear within months of appearing, and some have no websites and no phones, just a couple of guys willing to man a smoker or a pit like their dads did back in the day. Some of them even manage a little whole hog. There's a place that comes and goes just outside Royal too. Sometimes I'm lucky, sometimes not.

When people talk in capital letters about "barbecue" that's important; the four varieties are Tennessee/Memphis, Carolina, Texas, and Kansas City, as though other regions don't have something special or don't tie in to one of those traditions, influence it, and do things just as interesting and powerful within their culinary cultures. You can't have a real talk about barbecue in Missouri without talking about St. Louis's outstanding ribs, which are, in their own way, just as good as Kansas City's.

Likewise, if you start talking about Tennessee's barbecue culture, its tangy tomato-based sauces, and its slow pit cooking, then you have to include North Alabama in that discussion. That's even before you get into the big names and look at the many connections that have been made between chefs here and there, let alone figure in the impact that a program like Fatback may potentially have on both states and the surrounding areas.

To skip Alabama and pretend that an artificial border exists whereby the food changes and its cultural roots are instantaneously different is to neglect an important part of what's going on with barbecue in this part of the country and the ties and cultural connections between one state line and the other.

I've listed only a handful of restaurants for you to try here, but as with West Tennessee and Memphis, I urge you to stop at the little strip center places in small towns, the gas station barbecue joints, and the little places in the middle of nowhere. You'll have some amazing food—slow-cooked, tender, juicy pork at its best, not unlike Tennessee.

You'll also discover some distinctive Alabama stuff. White sauce on chicken, for example, one of the best things to come out of Big Bob Gibson's in Decatur.

But most important, remember that food doesn't change so much with the borders here. Remember that too when you're eating in places like Bowling Green, Kentucky, and Hernando, Mississippi. A region is more than state lines.

Western Kentucky

Kentucky barbecue is something close to Tennessee, but you'll find a few key differences—the largest of which is the absolute fondness for mutton that springs up in the west around Owensboro—yes, you read that right. This happens a lot in the western part of the state, where the wool industry has thrived for centuries.

The other big Kentucky staple is Burgoo, a stew of meat and vegetables that often has a little heat to it. The original usually involved game meats like venison but today is more likely pork, mutton, and chicken, plus potatoes, corn, beans, and such. It's kind of Kentucky's take on Brunswick stew, a common side item down here, and you'll find it on menus all over the state, including Lexington and Louisville. As with Tennessee, you'll find a lot of places by the side of the road and a little on the menu at every church picnic.

While we won't go into serious depth on Kentucky, here are a few places to try out that Burgoo, mutton, and some other good smoked proteins in the familiar style.

Moonlite Bar-B-Q Inn, 2840 W. Parrish Ave., Owensboro, KY 42301; (270) 684-8143; moonlite.com
A pretty spectacular buffet with a wide variety of barbecue, including mutton. This place has been around for decades with a great local reputation.

Old Hickory Bar-B-Q, 338 Washington Ave., Owensboro, KY 42301; (270) 926-9000; oldhickorybar-b-q.com
Another well-respected restaurant of long standing, with barbecue, burgers, catfish, and more. Try the mutton ribs.

Ole South Barbeque, 3523 Kentucky 54, Owensboro, KY 42303; (270) 926-6464
Popular lunch buffet here as well, and mutton is on the menu along with more familiar proteins, plus ribs, catfish, and more.

Also consider checking out Owensboro's own International Bar-B-Q Festival in May (bbqfest.com). There's plenty to do, and you'll find mutton competition as well as chicken, pork, and ribs. If your tastes run to mutton, I really think this is a fun side trip. Heck, it's a fun side trip regardless.

Big Bob Gibson's

1715 Sixth Ave. SE (US 31), Decatur, AL 35601, (256) 350-6969; 2520 Danville Rd. SW, Decatur, AL 35603, (256) 350-0404; bigbobgibson.com

North Alabama's barbecue traditions are very similar to those of southern Tennessee. Back in the 1920s, "Big" Bob Gibson, a railroad employee, would spend his weekends cooking up pork and chicken in hand-dug pits in his yard, feeding friends and family. His cookouts got so popular that he began selling his barbecue, and in 1925 he opened his restaurant. His family still owns and operates it today, with Chris Lilly at the helm (he married into the family). Over the generations, other family members migrated off to Huntsville and other locales and started their own barbecue places.

Big Bob Gibson's is all about meat—pork shoulder, chicken, brisket, turkey, and ribs all have a place on the menu. What's really special here is the chicken in Alabama white sauce, a peppery, tangy flavor unfamiliar to many outside the region. Big Bob's lets every chicken they cook sit in a bit of it before chopping, and there's more on the table for you to add—it's a signature taste, and you can order it online.

The award-winning red sauce, developed for Memphis in May between 1995 and 1997 and a first-prize winner there, is traditional to the region and recommended for pork and ribs. There's an assortment of house sauces, and each deserves consideration—including North Carolina vinegar and cayenne-based style and a mustard-based one.

At Big Bob Gibson's, the pie ladies come in even before the barbecue guys each morning, and you really don't want to leave without trying the pie. The coconut cream is especially superb, but the lemon chiffon, peanut butter, and pecan are all splendid. Don't leave without trying at least one.

Owner Chris Lilly also recommends trying their barbecue baked potato. "It's a meal in itself" with a huge roasting potato, sour cream, cheese, butter, chives, and barbecue.

Dreamland Barbecue

1427 14th Ave. S., Birmingham, AL, (205) 933-2133; 19 W. Oxmoor Rd., Birmingham, AL, (205) 943-0175; 5535 15th Ave. E., Tuscaloosa, AL, (205) 758-8135; 101 Tallapoosa St., Montgomery, AL, (334) 273-7427; and other area locations; dreamlandbbq.com

Former brick mason John "Big Daddy" Bishop opened the first Dreamland Café in Tuscaloosa, just outside Birmingham, in 1958, and it has grown to be a staple in the community. At this stage, it's a small-scale Alabama chain, with multiple locations fanning out from the Birmingham–Tuscaloosa area along I-59. Local

residents still love it, and folks who grew up in Birmingham still have a soft spot in their hearts for it. Catharine Newman, one of the founders of Nashville's Edley's, says that it was one of her inspirations and remains a favorite.

Back in the day, there was an abundance of food on the menu, but what it comes down to now is ribs, ribs, and ribs. "Dreamland is a staple around here; pretty much everyone in Birmingham has been there. It's very good," says Amy-Renee King, lifelong Birmingham resident and private chef. "They offer ribs only (slab or half slab) and sides, few sandwiches. Their ribs are amazing, though; my favorite ribs of all time, anywhere."

The sauce is thin, spicy, and totally delicious, according to patrons. It's one of the things that make Dreamland popular.

You'll find a number of side items on the menu again, of late, but what people come here for is the meat, both dining in and taking out. (Catering is also available.)

If you dine in, there's beer to be had, domestic and imported, mostly bottles.

Most of my friends favor the West Oxmoor Road location, but the quality is consistent across stores, and if you love a good rib, you aren't going to be disappointed.

Full Moon BBQ

525 25th St. S., Birmingham, AL 35233, (205) 324-1007; 337 Valley Ave., Birmingham, AL 35209, (205) 945-9997; 4635 US 280, Birmingham, AL 35242, (205) 991-7328; 1434 McFarland Blvd. E., Tuscaloosa, AL 35404, (205) 366-3555; and other area locations; fullmoonbbq.com

Full Moon is the brainchild of David and Joe Maluff, brothers who have built a small barbecue empire in the area and managed to keep it all magically delicious as they expanded to a total of nine stores in north-central Alabama. Keeping with tradition, the Full Moon restaurants believe in cooking over hickory in pits, slowly at low temperatures until everything is fall-off-the-bone fabulous. Full Moon has won plenty of awards, local and national, but it's the support of locals that keeps them in business.

Everything you find here is homemade, from the proteins coming out of the barbecue pits to the really delicious little cookies that complement your meal. (When I was doing a food tour of Alabama a couple of years back, during the state's Year of Alabama Food, those cookies were on their list of top 100 things to enjoy in the state.)

Order in or take out, start with the pork sandwich or the three-bone rib sandwich. There are several barbecue salad options, including a Greek salad with pulled chicken if you want to go light but not miss out on the barbecue.

You can get smoked quarter chickens, and Full Moon offers leg-thigh quarters if you like—something less common these days but excellent if you like dark meat.

As with most of the barbecue restaurants across the South, you can get nearly anything to go as well as dine in, including pints of sauce. The sides manage to echo the tradition—slaw, potato salad, baked beans, French fries, and the like—hearty support for the main course.

You've got the tough choice between Bud Light and Miller Light if you're in need of a cold one to sip with your ribs. Otherwise, look for soft drinks and sweet tea.

Saw's BBQ

1008 Oxmoor Rd., Birmingham, AL 35209, (205) 879-1937 (Homewood neighborhood); SAW's Soul Kitchen—Avondale, 215 41st St. S., Birmingham, AL 35222, (205) 591-1409; SAW's Juke Joint—Crestline, 1115 Dunston Ave., Birmingham AL 35213, (205) 745-3920; sawsbbq.com

At the risk of scatological humor, SAW's takes its name from founder Mike Wilson, courtesy of an old nickname, "Sorry Ass Wilson"—but there's zero that's sorry about SAW's in any of its locations. The North Carolina native studied at the University of Alabama, Birmingham, and made a career for himself as a chef while studying the ins and outs of Alabama barbecue on his own. In 2009, he purchased the former Broadway Barbecue in Homewood (a neighborhood with fine culinary and arts credentials) and opened up. He followed with SAW's Soul Kitchen (with Brandon Cain), just down the street from the pretty

The Chains: Whitt's Barbecue

Cooked over hickory wood low and slow, Whitt's (whittsbarbecue.com) is a North Alabama barbecue tradition. Dating to the late 1960s, Whitt's came to be when bricklayer Floyd Whitt devoted himself to a hobby: building his own barbecue pits in the Tennessee River valley around Decatur and Athens. He experimented his way into what he decided was a perfect pit concept, and he and his wife, Laura, began cooking up great pork. The taste went over so well with friends and neighbors that before long, the couple found themselves in the barbecue business.

Whitt's meat is still cooked the same way, using a basting sauce, slow and low over hickory coals. It's also still a family business, though the founders have passed on, spreading across North Alabama into Tennessee and across the region. Family members still hold a number of franchises in the area, including into Middle Tennessee.

Whitt's franchises are frequently more drive-through than sit-down, but that's not a bad thing. Pork, chicken, beef, and turkey are all available, as are ribs, and with them come a small number of the classic sides: baked beans, coleslaw, and potato salad. Don't look for a long menu of sides or a lot of fancy additions to the menu.

The prices are seriously affordable—as of this writing, you could get a family pack with 2 pounds of meat, buns, slaw and chips for about $25. Stuffed potatoes, meat or no meat, can be had, along with Brunswick stew. For dessert, there's an assortment of pies or cookies.

My Decatur friends Jean and Ken Hovey swear by Whitt's as the drive-through of choice, and Jean (better known as one-half the real-life version of romance writer Alicia Hunter Pace, along with Stephanie Jones) will never steer you wrong on good food.

The Nashville area has seen Whitt's proliferate since the late 1970s as well, so the franchise has a long history well outside of its Athens, Alabama, origins. At this point, much of the MidSouth region has Whitt's as part of its faster food options (as opposed to "fast food" because the barbecue is indeed still prepared the slow way, cooking for hours).

If you're on the go and just want a quick drive-through experience, Whitt's is a good decision.

delightful Avondale Brewery in 2012, and now has the Juke Joint in Crestline as well (with partners Doug Smith and Taylor Hicks—the *American Idol* guy).

The original SAW's is a little neighborhood place that's constantly packed with people. My friends Amy-Renee and Diana, who live in Homewood and who introduced me, say it's the kind of place a television producer might have dreamed up given the description "Alabama barbecue joint." Amy's husband Stephen is even more forceful about his fondness for it.

Both the white and the red sauces rock. Try the collard greens and the potato salad on the side of your pork sandwich or your chicken sandwich with white sauce. The banana pudding is pretty much the quintessence of southern banana pudding, so save a little room if you can. While you'll find ribs on the menu, don't look for brisket, bologna, or any of the newfangled trends that have spilled beyond Memphis.

The filled baked potatoes should also be on your list of things to try, especially the loaded potato with pork, chicken, bacon, and green onions, topped with barbecue sauce.

If you're a fan of the sauce, rest easy; you can order it online from the website. Catering is available. Closed Sunday.

(On a side note, I'm told to let you know that Dreamcakes Bakery next door to SAW's is worth a visit to grab sweets to take home when you've already had your meal and banana pudding.)

The Festival Circuit

If you're at all serious about barbecue, at some point in your life you need to get to a competition or two. That said, there are a wide variety of competitions out there, and not all of them are created equal. In this region, your options range from very small scale and local to enormous productions, like the Jack Daniel's Invitational and the granddaddy of them all, Memphis in May, which sees the city's streets fill with tens of thousands of people single-mindedly obsessing about barbecue. Depending on what your tastes run to, there is absolutely something out there to fit your needs. Most people don't realize that even some of the very large competitions have a "backyard" category that allows newcomers to get their feet wet and find out if it's for them, without the major expenses that a full-time team might expect.

If you look across Tennessee, North Alabama, and Kentucky, you'll find festivals and competitions going on from spring to fall, with most heavily weighted in the late spring and early fall, given the weather conditions of our region. Let's face it: No one wants to cook over an open pit or even with a smoker in 95°F August heat and, most of the time, high humidity. That means look for lots of events in April and May and again in September and early October.

Wonderful Small Time: Chester County

Pat Martin, when I interviewed him early on in the course of writing this book, told me that for his money, the best competition was the **Chester County** festival, which really did let a bunch of folks who truly wanted to kick back, have fun, and smoke some hog do what they did best, without the insane pressures of the big time—but still with the kind of pride in ability that comes from excelling.

"It's really old school, there's no circuit involved here," says Martin. "They build a bunch of block pits, and all the old guys set up all night and cook these pigs." It is, he adds, very much unadulterated by today's formal barbecue competition ethos. "Just whole hog, West Tennessee–style barbecue."

The difference at the really small festivals is that most of the time the competitors do it for themselves to underline and prove their ability. You won't see $100,000 rigs pull up with professional traveling teams, but you'll see both restaurant owners and hobbyists sitting up to the wee hours and working to smoke the best meats they know how, bringing in the traditions of their fathers and grandfathers.

The next step up from there are local festivals that are more centered on adjudicated judging—you'll find quite a few that now insist on Kansas City Barbecue Society (KCBS)-trained judges and rules. That's important because it asks the judges to maintain a style that doesn't always favor taste over other qualities, including presentation and texture.

What KCBS doesn't do is favor a regional style over others, lest you worry that, because it's Kansas City, they expect Kansas City barbecue every time. What it does do is focus specifically on four categories: ribs, pork, chicken, and brisket.

When you go to a competition like, for example, Jack Daniel's or Memphis in May, the judging is being done to KCBS or Memphis Barbecue Network standards. With a small competition like Chester County, that's not the case.

Family Fun: Barbecue on the River

A terrific regional event that doesn't entirely rely on KCBS standards but does pull in large crowds is **Barbecue on the River** in Paducah, Kentucky. According to cofounder Susie Coiner, the judging teams are made up of one certified judge, then the remaining four members of each judging team include a sponsor of the festival (a "friend of barbecue"), a food industry member, a local "celebrity," and a dignitary, such as a local judge, the mayor, or someone who has a prominent position in the city. From their perspective, that allows for many different impressions to impact the final results.

Barbecue on the River is a recent addition to the region, begun in 1995 with Coiner's family, who had a new business in the area at the time. They were looking to get involved more in the community, and a chance conversation with employees from the newly opened nearby casino brought up the notion of a barbecue competition.

Susie then luckily paired with Ro Morse of the Paducah Convention and Visitors Bureau, and together they got the support of the bureau. After a little research and some deal making with local companies to supply the pork and chicken for the festival, a community charity fund-raiser was born—one that supported the area's history of barbecue. Almost 20 years later, it's still going strong.

The biggest difference between this festival and many of the larger ones is that teams sell directly to the public, so you can come in and buy and sample to your heart's content. The health department inspects the vendors daily. U.S.

Foods is now the primary supplier and sponsor, with teams meeting 3 weeks in advance and placing their meat orders.

What this also means is that amateurs and professionals are competing with each other, something you won't see at a lot of the bigger competitions. And I can't stress how rare it is that guests get to purchase and eat entrants' food. At a typical big competition, this kind of vending just doesn't exist.

At the first event, 16 teams sold out of their products by noon at the 1-day event. This year, there were more than 40 competitors, and they even raised some $448,000 for local charities. The event categories are chicken, ribs, pork shoulders, and whole hog. You can enter just 1 category or all 4, but you'd best enter all 4 if you hope to be grand champion.

Besides barbecue, you have a chance to wander down "Fixin's Row" and find desserts galore. And the atmosphere is very much state fair level of fun—there's a whole weekend of live music and entertainment, a beer garden, and 100 or so non–food vendors selling everything from artisan crafts to cheesy sunglasses.

By the end of the weekend, they've fed 40,000 or so guests. I know several Nashville barbecue fans who wouldn't miss this one for the world. It's a good time without some of the pressures of the more historical and sanctioned competitions. Fun is the order of the day, and if you go home hungry, it's your own fault.

High Style: Jack Daniel's Invitational World Championship

By contrast, the **Jack Daniel's Invitational World Championship** is something else, something the entire tiny hamlet of Lynchburg comes out and celebrates. Judging is done to KCBS standards, and the contest sees itself as akin to a true world series of barbecue. It's a wonderful, joyously carnival experience with 25,000 people sweeping into a town of less than 7,000 where the smell of whiskey that haunts it every day gives way to the smell of smoke and meat cooking.

"I rank our competition as one of the best of the best," says Steve May, director of the visitor's center at Jack Daniel's—the guy who runs the tourist side of the business for Jack Daniel's. "Passion goes into the event. Competitors aspire to be part of it, and few get the chance; it's hard to get in. People—both competitors and guests—are really thrilled to be here."

Of course, you find out that most of the regular residents are pretty happy to participate in one way or another as well; some even qualify as judges to lend a hand.

The festival came about because a quarter century ago, the company wanted a way to give back to the local population for their support and to say thank you. At the time, formal barbecue competitions were at what May calls a "preteen" stage across the whole region, and Jack Daniel's helped to formalize the concept, all the while celebrating the heritage of barbecue.

At the time, there wasn't a structured "world championship," so they decided to define what that might look like for themselves. They wanted teams who had won a 25-or-more team event, with a state endorsement or governor's proclamation making them official. They made it invitational, inviting teams from all over the world, helping to build an out-of-country structure in some places as they went about it. The idea is that you've got to prove yourself to get to come to this one.

The first year saw just under 50 teams, and 2013 featured 98: 76 from the US and 22 from abroad. Applying KCBS rules, teams enter 1 or more of 4 categories: chicken, ribs, pork, and beef brisket. The typical team is professional or semiprofessional, one that's competed all over. When they ride into town, you know it, with their dedicated trucks and heavy-duty pickups hauling trailers with high-grade smokers. There's some real money that's been poured into the equipment you see here.

"We're seen as a premiere event," says May. "It's a big deal to be invited."

When you come to the Jack, expect huge amounts of traffic, but roll down your windows because it smells like heaven. The environment is super family friendly; Lynchburg is a dry town in a dry county, so there's no alcohol for sale at all, anywhere, unless you're doing the distillery tour and buying a souvenir package (not to say there isn't anything in the competition's coolers—as regular judge Chris Chamberlain says, there's a reason why big refillable mugs of lemonade are some of the most popular things for sale at the Jack—but don't look for the beer tent or try to buy a cocktail).

If you're going to be in Tennessee in October, I'd recommend trying to make this one. Unlike the smaller festivals, don't look to the teams to feed you, but there are vendors who'll make sure you don't leave hungry. Make reservations in advance—there are no short-notice hotel rooms to be had for miles.

Judging at the Jack

My friend and fellow food writer Chris Chamberlain (author of *The Southern Foodie's Guide to the Pig*) sat down to talk with me a few days after judging the 2014 Jack Daniel's Invitational and shared a bit of what it's like during the heady process of picking the best of the best at one of the most high-powered competitions in the country.

This is the fourth year in a row he's been fortunate enough to judge. Chris has become pretty familiar with the KCBS rules that govern the process, and he leads off by making me understand the first thing to know about the Jack is that the food quality is exceptional.

"Generally things are getting 8 to 9 points on the 2 to 9 scale. And that's far from average; people at this level of competition know better than to do things like, say, start their fires with lighter fluid because they understand how errors like that affect taste."

For the judges, that makes it even harder; consistent quality, plus meeting the KCBS standards, underlines that participants are moving toward what Chris refers to as a "competitive mean"—an across-the-board similarity in style, taste, and texture, all at an exceptional level of preparation, to meet the exacting requirements of the competition.

The variation comes mostly, Chris says, because it is an "international"; that is, they're cycling in teams from all over the world each year, and he says, "The results from those teams may be totally out of left field. Generally things are so consistent that looking at my box as a judge, 4 or 5 of the 7 ribs from the same rack: They had the right shape; they were perfectly sauced. But talking to a friend of mine later, he had the same situation, except that one of his was very different, completely random—it was cooked to grayness, with heavy salt and pepper—obviously from someone outside the states whose take at home meant they won that contest, even if it doesn't resemble what's expected at this one."

Notable about 2014, he tells me, was ideal weather. "These were pretty forgiving conditions; there were no cold, wet nights to deal with." He explains, for those who don't follow the barbecue circuit, that the whole experience is often

(continued)

about spending the weekend living in tents or RVs and cooking the whole time. It's exhausting but full of conviviality.

"Bad weather conditions give a big advantage to the hyper professional teams that come in with the serious rigs. For the smaller guys who don't have the most competitive equipment, it can wreak havoc on your fire temperatures when the winds hit the grill. This year, it was clear, in the low 60s at night, mid-70s and sunny during the day—pretty nice for October, and it made the barbecue better across the board."

So, I say, tell me what this whole judging experience is like.

"Well, getting there and back to Sewanee was a little nerve wracking on Friday," he says with a grin. "The Ragnar Relay was going on, so I had to compete at night on two-lane roads with hundreds of runners all the way home." Friday is made of fun, so Chris got to do a tasting with Jack Daniel's Master Distiller Jeff Arnett, and Rose Arnold of Arnold's Country Kitchen in Nashville also brought an impressive spread.

Saturday marks the start of true judging. Sign in takes place right at 10 a.m.; then, Chris says, they "kind of herd you" into a little pen through a cattle gate, where you look to find your table.

"Everyone gets an apron and a silver sharpie—with which you proceed to get everyone's signature on your apron because you've got regional celebrities and some well-known food people among your collection of judges." There follows a judges' meeting where the whole lot of them settle down for a recording reviewing the rules of KCBS barbecue (almost all major competitions depend on the KCBS rules or, less frequently, the Memphis Barbecue Network rules—you can find the KCBS rules for 2014 at kcbs.us/pdf/2014_rules.pdf).

For judges, there's no opportunity to fraternize with the team members on Saturday the way they might have during the Friday preliminaries.

"At my judging table, I was pretty lucky. I had Mike 'the Legend' Mills [celebrated pitmaster of 17th Street Barbecue, 17thstreetbarbecue.com]; a judge from North Alabama who'd been judging here for something like 22 years; a couple who'd been here for a year or two; and then a first-timer was so excited, he spent the beginning of the process just wondering 'how do I get to do this again?' Our table captains were a husband-and-wife team from North Alabama who were just great—they made a lot of jokes but were very professional."

Together, Chris and his table judged the 4 standard categories—chicken, pork, ribs, and brisket—plus, as the table captains promised, "we'll make sure you get a little ancillary"—those categories being sauce, dessert, and chef's choice.

The day runs long and busy, from 10 a.m. to 3 p.m. "I tried to make sure I was ready for it all this year," Chris says ruefully. "It added up to about 2 pounds of eating—it's a marathon, not a sprint. I'm much better at pacing myself than I used to be, though I have to say, I didn't seriously think about consuming anything again for a day and a half."

That's with a core of 6 judges each at 14 or 15 tables, plus a few volunteers roped in to sample desserts and the like.

Judges take on one category at a time, starting with chicken. "The Jack is unusual in that you're getting both white and dark meat," says Chris. "Although smoked wings technically qualify as 'white' meat—which is a little different—most of what you get is a uniform piece of chicken thigh that's been put in a muffin tin with butter and smoked, so it looks a little like a hockey puck but is completely tender and delicious."

Then come the ribs. "Ours were all terrific and pretty uniform—all at 8 or 9 points." Third is pulled pork—shoulder or butt, not whole hog. Finally, there is brisket.

"The brisket was surprisingly good this year," Chris comments. "Brisket isn't really a southern meat, well, except for Texas, but it's growing in popularity in competition down here." (He and I have a long secondary conversation about the economics of beef in the current drought-impacted climate in Texas and Oklahoma, how it affects us in Tennessee, and how that affects the larger barbecue world—especially when trend makes a traditionally cheap cut like brisket suddenly expensive.)

The ancillary categories offer up a sauce that must be made with Jack Daniel's Tennessee Whiskey—"that's all pretty subjective, we have to consider things like mouth feel and how chunky it may be and whether it's ultimately a good use of Jack Daniels."

The chef's choice category allows especially the international teams to show off dishes from their homelands, cooking anything, with the traditional rule set going out the window. "I had a brisket Reuben that was absolutely fantastic; the brisket would have placed well on its own," says Chris.

(continued)

If the regular judges have tapped out, the dessert category lets volunteers participate in their places. "We were joined by one that happened to have been my table captain the day before, when I did my refresher KCBS class," says Chris. "I'm always surprised by what turns up; it can be as simple as cookies or as crazy as a flaming volcano of chocolate. Desserts don't have to be completely created on-site; the teams can bring them in in coolers and finish them in time for the competition.

What's important here is that all this is blind judging: You as judge have no idea whose cooking you taste in any competition. In KCBS, competitors simply turn in their boxes to be judged. Anyone caught marking their boxes in any way gets disqualified, making sure there is no chance a judge can know whose food they have in front of them.

The Memphis Barbecue Network adds a category whereby judges actually go visit each team's cook site, tasting the meat as it's being prepared. "That's kind of a dog-and-pony show," says Chris. "You get to present your space, your technique, literally everything, and the top make the finals."

"In 2014, what really stood out to you at the Jack?" I ask.

"Well, beyond the fact that things are still really progressing toward that 'competitive mean' I mentioned earlier, which does mean less variety in the long run, I think in the main four categories, the brisket just continues to get better every year.

"And if you're planning on coming, there are some things to know. With a competition like the Jack, unless you learn to be a judge, you pretty much need to be a member of a team to get most of the good food. With the health codes and everything surrounding most of these competitions, you're just not allowed to wander around and try things from the teams.

"That said, it's a fantastic experience to be a member of a team, you sleep in tents, it's all the convivial atmosphere of cooking, and there's the stress of competition and turning things in on top of it. But really, I think more people ought to try it. Most don't know there's a 'backyard' type of competition at many of these festivals that lets amateurs really have a chance to do it for themselves.

"And finally, this is just a special event; you know you'll have a great time. The hospitality is first rate."

The Big Moment: Memphis in May

The big daddy of festivals around here is **Memphis in May,** an extraordinary convergence of the epitome of barbecue preparation with a city that has defined its heritage and brand with two things: barbecue and music. If the Jack takes over a small town, Memphis in May sweeps into a city and builds an almost Mardi Gras sense of celebration.

"It started small and tapped a nerve in the city," says Memphis in May CEO Jim Holt. "It's grown from very humble beginnings in 1978 to become the most prestigious barbecue competition in the world, one that attracts a national and global audience. It reinforces the city's reputation as the barbecue capital of the world. There are only two cities in the world that are recognized for their barbecue: Memphis and Kansas City. There are only two regions (not cities), the Carolinas and Texas, that are recognized as barbecue regions."

Memphis in May is actually a full month's worth of weekend-long celebrations, of music, the arts, and more. The barbecue aspect takes up just one of those weekends, but it has come to symbolize some of the best of the best of the barbecue firmament.

PHOTO COURTESY OF MEMPHIS IN MAY

Holt is right: Over the past 30 years, Memphis in May has helped solidify the notion of Memphis barbecue. The competition helps define the city's character to the world, underlining its great culinary traditions even as it draws between 60,000 and 80,000 visitors and an average of 250 teams to be strenuously judged using KCBS standards.

Early in the week, any number of hospitality events take place as the teams are setting up—some are hosted by the teams themselves for family and friends, some by corporate and team sponsors. Holt says one of the ways to know you're really possessed of social status in the city is by counting the number of invites you receive to these events.

The drinking and dancing run Thursday into Friday, but late-night Friday the teams get focused, the cooking really goes down, and the party atmosphere is replaced by a commitment to serious cookery. (Some of us who know teams are pretty happy to sit around and watch prep and drink a beer with the guys before the heavy work gets going, trust me.)

One thing to remember—this isn't a contest for newbies who want to try their hands against the big guys. The level of competition amongst the grill masters has grown exponentially over the years and continues to push the limits of skill.

"The champion grill masters and their highly technical and artistic approach to barbecue deservedly get a lot of attention," says Holt. But for those who are a little under the radar and looking to build both knowledge and skill, he adds, "Many people think they can walk in and compete with the best of the best. They can, through our starter division—Patio Porkers. However, this contest isn't for rookies—it is truly the World Championship of Barbecue."

At Memphis in May, amid all the merriment, it's important to remember again that this level isn't an all-you-can-eat buffet, Holt points. When you come in, the teams are focused solely on cooking and getting those results to the judges. Some teams may offer you a sample, but most probably won't. But it's an incredible spectacle—your eyes and ears and sense of taste can hit sensory overload.

What you should know is that in Memphis, there's a good barbecue joint on every corner. If you're going, for heaven's sake, take time to eat at the places listed in this book—and find a few new ones as well.

Barbecue Festival Guide

If you want to catch up on the world of competition barbecue, here are some options. Make sure you check out details to make sure the festival matches your needs. Not all festivals allow guests to buy or try samples of competition meats, for example, while others encourage it. Check out all the details before you plan your trip. If you're not up for 50,000 or more people filling downtown Memphis, some of the smaller festivals may really be for you, where you can relax and talk to the pitmasters a little.

My serious barbecue fan friends swear by the tiny Chester County Festival—a West Tennessee–style celebration of serious slow cooking. Pat Martin tells me it's the thing that restores your faith in barbecue. For myself, I love Memphis in May, but that doesn't mean a smaller, local, relaxed festival can't be an amazing experience.

Alabama
Barbecue for Building
April, Birmingham
Benefits Habitat for Humanity
bbqforbuilding.com

Cotton Pickin' BBQ Cookoff
May, Hartselle
hartsellechamber.org

Hot Barbecue, Cool Blues
July, Tuscumbia
cityoftuscumbia.org

Tri-State Barbecue Festival
April, Dothan
tristatebarbecue.com

Whistlestop Weekend
May, Huntsville
rocketcitybbq.com

Tennessee

Bloomin' Barbecue and Bluegrass
May, Sevierville
bloominbbq.com

Bluegrass and Barbecue
May through June, Pigeon Forge/Dollywood
dollywood.com

Chester County Barbecue Festival
September, Henderson
chestercountychamber.com/chamber-events

Dumplin' Valley Bluegrass Festival
September, Kodak
dumplinvalleybluegrass.com

High on the Hog Festival
April, Winchester
highonthehogfestival.com

The Jack Daniel's World Invitational Barbecue Championship
September, Lynchburg
jackdaniels.com

Memphis in May
Downtown Memphis, May
memphisinmay.org

Music City Festival and Barbecue Championship
September, Nashville
musiccitybbqfestival.com

National Muscadine Festival and Barbecue Competition
Sweetwater, September
nationalmuscadinefestival.com

Kentucky
Barbecue on the River
Paducah, September
bbqontheriver.org

So You Want to Be a Barbecue Star

All barbecue chefs don't decide to make a living in barbecue. I've come across plenty who are content to make great food following family traditions simply for the joy of it and to share with friends and relations. And there are any number of competitive teams with no ambition to start a restaurant of their own or to be featured on the Food Network. But one thing is true in the South—someone in your circle is devoted to barbecue, probably many "someones."

As I've pointed out before, the thing about barbecue competitions is that not all of them require you to be a serious contender. Most of them, large and small, have a category specifically for backyard chefs to get a handle on how the process works. If you think you might like to try the whole competition experience, I really encourage you to try it out from this perspective. If nothing else, it's just good fun.

The Professionals

I've heard **Pat Martin**'s origin stories over beer many times. He learned how to cook whole hog living in West Tennessee and going to college at Freed-Hardeman, and it sank deeply into the fiber of his being. He gave it a go as something other than a barbecue chef for any number of years, but it never quite worked out. I secretly think his incredible wife, Martha, breathed a sigh of relief when he finally found himself at the literal crossroads out in Nolensville—like Saul on the way to Damascus, Pat Martin saw the light.

He opened up his tiny joint, and the sky became the limit. Then he opened the bigger place across the street, then locations in Mount Juliet and the Belmont neighborhood in Nashville—somehow maintaining the quality (and probably getting very little sleep). As with many of the best, there just came a time when he knew where his future lay and, with it, the art of preserving the heritage of barbecue.

PHOTO COURTESY OF PAT MARTIN, MARTIN'S BBQ JOINT

Left to right: Pat Martin, Tandy Wilson, and Tyler Brown

Every now and then, he'll grizzle at me about 6 years of hard work, a few more gray hairs, a few more pounds—then he'll start talking about expanding the smoker and having a bigger pit so he can maybe cook whole goat and other wonders, and he'll smile and be transformed. He loves his barbecue life. Can't say I blame him one bit.

I've known **Carey Bringle** less well and for a lesser amount of time. I met him during a weekend fund-raising for Share Our Strength, as he barbecued a fantastic lunch for a crowd of us who were visiting—mostly journalists and chefs—at the amazing heritage farm kept by Chef Tyler Brown and the staff at the Capitol Grille at Nashville's Hermitage Hotel. It took a couple of years for him to get his signature Peg Leg Porker restaurant open from there, but no one doubted it would come—and be exceptional.

Carey had a 20-year history on serious barbecue teams behind him: Hog Wild and then his Peg Leg Porker team. He's a walking historian of Memphis in May, and he learned his first lessons from his uncle, a guy who competed at the first Memphis in May.

"I started on my first real team in 1989," he says. "The Rolling Wonder Pigs. We were quite the party crew, so much so that we eventually got kicked out, and so we sat out a year, then came back as Hog Wild. Ernie Mellor and Tripp Murray were the captains—they've both made good names for themselves; I was a founding member. I learned a whole lot from those two. We took second in shoulder that year. Had a grease fire in the pit, thought we'd be disqualified, but we got second. We had two more second-place finishes in the next few years."

After about 12 years, during which time he developed his own seasoning and sauce, he broke off and started the Peg Leg Porker Team. He is still set up next to the Hog Wild Team at Memphis in May. But as you've already read, Bringle brought his lifelong love of Memphis barbecue to a fantastic restaurant in Nashville, his Peg Leg Porker.

Both Pat and Carey exemplify the kind of guys who obsessed over barbecue long before the idea of restaurants and the kind of television attention they've since received ever occurred to them. And they're a big part of why Nashville is getting so much attention for its barbecue credentials. Without Pat and Carey, that wouldn't be happening. More important, perhaps, they also close a cultural gap, bringing Middle Tennessee together with West Tennessee and Memphis and reminding us that we're all in this fantastic world of outstanding barbecue together.

Barbecue on the River

Barbecue on the River stands out distinctively because the competitors are also vendors; they're not just there for the glory of the competition. **Darrell Scott,** a high school baseball coach, found himself involved that way, leading a team to raise money for his high school baseball club. The end result has managed to be pretty spectacular. When I spoke to Darrell, he was just 24 hours removed from the 2014 event and excited about the Ballard Baseball Boosters having taken first place in the chicken competition, third in pork shoulder, and fourth in ribs.

Given the size of the event, that's a pretty spectacular showing, but at the time I called him, Scott was already sitting at his desk with his score sheets in front of him, checking out the Internet for upgrades to grilling equipment for 2015. This isn't the first brush with success for the team he leads: Over the past 6 years, since they began participating, they've racked up three firsts and "eight or nine seconds and thirds," according to Scott. The only big issue now is whether to reexamine their own traditions and add whole hog into the mix; the only way to be considered for grand champion of the event, no matter how well you do otherwise, is to enter all four of the competition's juried categories.

"With our success, you have to think about adding it in," he says thoughtfully. "It's the only way you get considered for the grand prize, no matter how well your other entries have done. We've been good, it might be time we did it all."

Scott says he's been barbecuing on his own for at least 15 to 20 years; that's the kind of barbecue you do for friends and family in the backyard. For several years prior to his participation, those same acquaintances had been trying to convince him to go up and try his hand, but he didn't have the interest in doing it without a real solid team behind him. "It's also such huge volume, what with serving the public, I just didn't have all the stuff myself to make it happen," he admits.

Unlike the other big-name competitions in this region, Barbecue on the River encourages its entrants to open up their booths and sell to the folks coming in the gate. That means that an astonishingly high amount of food goes out.

When his baseball booster friends encouraged him to help them out at Barbecue on the River as a fund-raiser to replace two smaller ones, it provided the opportunity he needed. Before stepping into it, he hadn't done much at all in the way of competition barbecue. Even now, Scott does only a little 1-day competition event in his county at a Harvest Days festival besides his participation in Barbecue on the River. So far, he has no impetus to move on to Jack Daniel's or Memphis in May. "I don't really do the circuit, it's not my thing, but I enjoy this," he says.

However, a festival remains just as demanding for him as the larger events. Although Barbecue on the River doesn't officially open until Thursday, they're already hard at work on Tuesday setting up and on Wednesday preparing hundreds of sack lunches, which really means they cook virtually all night on Wednesday—well before they get going for the competition itself. Darrell Scott admits that those 525 sack lunches this year made it pretty hectic.

His own role is as lead chef on the project, cooking the meats mostly in the evenings, while his crew mans things during the day as he goes home, cleans up, naps a little, takes care of the needs of his real job, and then comes back by 4 or 5 p.m. reenergized and ready to go late into the night. Someone has to be on-site all the time, not only manning the booth also but making sure all preparations go as needed.

By the time Friday night comes, Scott is ready to skip all the sleep for the weekend. All the formal competition is on Saturday, so he's making sure, for example, that the chicken goes on at 3 a.m. and the ribs at 3:35 a.m. so that they can be ready the next morning to be delivered to the judges. The chicken gets judged at 9 a.m., the ribs at 10 a.m., and the pork shoulder at 11 a.m. "I've just got to get them done by the time to turn them in. Wow, it's a hectic day. I just don't sleep Friday. I get home Friday morning about noon, take a quick nap, then I'm back at 2 p.m. and won't sleep again until I get home somewhere around 10:30 on Saturday night."

Why then, I ask him, does he put himself through all this? He laughs, "Because it's so much fun, even with the long hours. I see so many people I haven't seen in years, poking their heads into the booth and talking, or people I see once a year. I'm also lucky enough to have a great group to work with, and I know they appreciate what I bring to it, that they find my knowledge valuable. And it's such a fantastic feeling when you win; you know you've accomplished something big."

So, is there a secret to the win, I wonder?

"We don't do a lot of fancy," Darrell Scott declares. "It's 'old timey' barbecue, not a lot of Memphis rubs or goopy sauces; we focus on good charcoal, and we're very consistent. There's just not a lot to mess with. My best advice to anyone wanting to step into this game is that while it's really scary at first, when you see just how big the festival's gotten, it's worth doing. Just remember that 'keep it simple' rule. Don't get intimidated, keep it simple."

He says his success is also predicated on the fact that the team really zeroes in on the barbecue. "We do make a sauce, but we don't enter that; and no sides for us either, although there are categories for sides."

Scott is one of the guys in the middle—not yet on to big ribs and big-time competitions like Jack Daniel's but well beyond the backyard. Once a year or so, he puts everything he's got, including an investment in good equipment, into feeding the crowds and pleasing the judges at one of the biggest events in the region.

The Amateurs—Ordinary Guys

Other guys who never enter the professional world still often have profound stories to offer of their barbecue quests. A few examples of the ordinary Tennessee barbecue amateur experts I rely on are my friends **Vincent Farone** and **Carson Reed** and my dad, without whom I probably still wouldn't get what goes into it all. They don't aim to win at Memphis in May; they just want to carry on the age-old traditions and get it right—kind of like most of us.

In the South, cooking barbecue is something a lot of people do. For years, it was a thing passed from father to son, although a growing number of female pitmasters and home cooks have now delved in deeply.

Vincent is a Chattanooga native who now lives in Knoxville. He has always been the chef among our closest circle of friends, holding annual culinary events at his home and bringing us all in for "Lamb-apalooza" and "Waffle Iron Chef" and "Sausage Fest" (yes, really, we all had to present dishes made with sausage—good times).

But Vincent is one of the few guys I know who decided he was going to master whole hog cooking with a pit dug in the backyard for the heck of it, and he did so—painstakingly, over years of experimentation with getting everything just right. I've watched Vincent sit next to a pit for something like 16 straight hours trying to get it right, checking religiously on his fire and his coals. This kind of thing underlines just what it takes for the guys who make their living this way and the reason there are so few cooking whole hog in the professional world any longer. It's grueling, hard work.

There's nothing like watching a crowd of hungry people rip into meat freshly chopped from a pig that's cooked steadily for 18 hours—fingers greasy and blackened from bits of crispy skin we've torn off. It might as well be a thousand years ago—barbecue is an archetypal experience.

And so Vincent in recent years (aided by our friends Sean Reisz and Justin Yodis) has reminded me of the sheer joy that can come from the act of cooking as a long and slow process and inadvertently perhaps tapped in to the thing that drew Pat Martin in as he learned the secrets of whole hog cooking in West Tennessee—the intensity of the experience, the work, and the bonding that happens when you're the girl setting a bunch of chickens up on beer cans to cook around the hog on the pit.

Vincent's latest efforts, now that he's got whole hog down, involve charcuterie. I've already tasted the first fruits of this, and I can't wait to see where it goes. I'm not entirely sure he isn't headed down a similar path as Carey and Pat, albeit more slowly. His wife, Kathy, a lawyer who has plenty of artistic skill of her own, will doubtless encourage him.

The day he opens a place, I think the entire city of Knoxville will flock to his door.

By contrast, I am fairly sure that being a chef is not on Carson Reed's mind right now. He has a solid day job, a gorgeous baby daughter, and a lovely wife who appreciates his culinary efforts too.

"I'm a home cook," he says. "I don't know necessarily what makes what I do special, but I know what makes it good. Barbecue is a southern tradition, and I wanted to learn how to do it, to tie in to that historic tradition, all my life."

Carson's oldest barbecue memories date back to his childhood near White Bluff, Tennessee (he's the guy who introduced me to Carl's Perfect Pig). He tells the story of his father taking him periodically to a small, largely African American town nearby in Cheatham County where they'd have weekend barbecues—cooking whole hog, chickens, goats, and chitlins.

"There was a little cinder-block pit, a little store there," he says. "The chitlins were cooked over open fire. My dad ate those, and I ate barbecue." He still also remembers his dad and his friends staying up all night, cooking 8 or 10 pork shoulders at a time.

Carson typically finds the piece of meat he's looking to cook and tinkers with his own rub, researching the style he's aiming for through cookbooks and the Internet.

"My wood of choice is applewood, and I'm not a lot about brine or injecting. I usually like to make my own sauce." He adds that he'd like to hear more people talking about sauces—that discussion is usually left out of the television shows.

Barbecue Is Love

The point of all this is that for most of the barbecue chefs I know, some who have spent their whole lives in Tennessee and some who have traveled a bit, barbecue is both an art and a science. They've spent whole lives watching dads and friends and built their own methods and mastered the craft—and still they seek out a level of perfection.

It's so often commented on that women in particular, especially of my grandmother's generation, showed their love through food. As far as I can figure, that's not limited to women, and a lot of rough-and-tumble guys show their love through barbecue. That's not to deny the incredible power of female pitmasters like Melissa Cookston, Helen Turner, and Molly James, just to point out that men are just as capable of expressing love through food as women—and barbecue often provides the mode of expression.

Hand me a sandwich, or I might tear up.

Since I've known Carson, his social media profile has been dedicated to his quest for incredible barbecue, and he has succeeded at a rate that would give a barbecue team a sense of pride.

He's not yet tried the whole hog or whole goat (that's next on his agenda), and he'd really like to look at a smokehouse and making his own hams.

I always think that on some level, this kind of devotion is more the rule in the South than the exception. We still maintain a deep cultural connection with our food.

My own first experiences are courtesy of my dad, **Colonel Joe Stewart** (US Air Force, retired). He had a long career, first in the air force and then in corporate America, that allowed him to take his understanding of southern barbecue, translate it through other experience around the world, and bring it back here to perfect.

My first memories of my dad barbecuing are twofold. One is being about 4 years old, back in the 1970s, when we lived in Athens, and going to the beach where folks from his squadron and some Greeks would be cooking lamb and kid over coals on the beach. The other is later, watching him and my uncle Bill Howell cook up an incredible number of Boston butts to feed our extended family (my grandparents on Dad's side came from families of 12 and 13 kids, so my family is enormous) at South Carolina reunions.

Dad's earliest memories of barbecue date back to the 1950s, going as a child with his father to Richmond, Virginia, from the Tidewater area and stopping at a little joint on the way to the ballpark.

"It was the classic, pulled pork, coleslaw, hot sauce, a soft bun," he says. My mom swears that the same joint stayed open under different owners for decades, and my grandparents always insisted on stopping there when in Richmond.

For himself, my dad recalls himself as a young lieutenant in the 1960s in Savannah, Georgia, trying to cook ribs on a grill and being too impatient, getting the grill too hot, and burning them. "I watched a lot of guys over the years who did it better and learned a little patience," he says.

Without thought to Rendezvous now, he talks about what he learned from the Greeks. "They cooked a lot over olive wood coals, using rotating spits, and their spices and sauces were very different, but they made a whole lot of good food." At that point, he says, the dominant spice he used was Turkish paprika, anywhere from hot to mild and sweet, blended with oregano and a bit of mustard powder, and the blends of paprika were very much in parallel to our love of chiles in turn back here.

These days, I go to Dad before anyone else for barbecue. He's just cooking for us, but that's just fine in my book (he could open a place if he wanted to, but he has other interests). "I don't like commercial charcoal," he says. "I use applewood and hickory. I finally learned to start a fire soon enough and to wait for it to get a real bed of coals to the temperature I wanted."

He still makes his own rubs, admitting he takes some inspiration from Emeril Lagasse on those and sometimes uses Emeril's Essence as an ingredient. "Those tastes and flavors seem right to me, after living in Georgia and Mississippi and frequent trips to New Orleans, then I add what I want, chilies, paprika, cayenne, mustard, salt, pepper. For the past 15 years or so, after plenty of trips out there on my Harley, I've been adding New Mexico green chilies to the mix."

Next on dad's agenda is perfecting his brisket.

RECITES

In the Kitchen & Around the Smoker

Everyone has their own take on smoking pork and whether to pull or chop. Here are a few really good recipes you can use to encourage folks to keep coming back for more at your own barbecue events in the backyard. Whether you're having a couple of buddies over to watch the big game and making a single pork butt or planning on a big spread for 100 close friends and family members, there's enough here to get you through.

Some of these are well known, some are old recipes passed down to friends and relatives, and a couple come from big-name restaurateurs, but all of them will please the people you have over for dinner.

Make sure you have plenty of sweet tea, Coca-Cola, and a tub full of cold beer on ice. But you knew that, right?

BLACK-EYED PEAS & GREENS WITH SAUSAGE

This recipe comes to me by way of my amazing friend Melissa Corbin, of Corbin in the Dell, (corbinin thedell.com). Melissa works diligently in the Middle Tennessee area to connect local food producers with commercial outlets, including restaurants—something I consider a very noble job. As she puts it, she supports "sustainable farmers and those who give a damn." Exactly: She has become one of my heroes for the work she does making a difference daily in our food community.

This particular recipe is one that's very appropriate for New Year as well as barbecue meals. Down here, you can't really have New Year without peas and greens, plus a little ham. Barbecue will no doubt make an acceptable substitute. **Serves 8–10**

Heat large skillet on high. Add olive oil, ½ teaspoon thyme, red pepper flake, and a crack or two of black pepper. Sauté onions and bacon until soft. Add garlic and ½ teaspoon salt for about 1 minute. The greens can now be tossed a little at a time. It will seem there is too many for your pan. Don't worry, as they cook down. Add ½ cup chicken broth as needed to get the pot "likker" going. Once the greens are cooked down, add balsamic vinegar and sugar. Cover and simmer for 5 minutes. Meanwhile, in a crock pot, stir together peas, tomatoes, 3½ cups chicken broth, ½ teaspoon thyme, ½ teaspoon salt, and a few cracks of black pepper. Pour in greens with likker and all. Gently fold in kielbasa. Crock pot should be up to ¾ full. If not, add just a little water. Cover and cook on high 3–4 hours, stir, and then turn on low until time to serve.

2 tablespoons olive oil
1 teaspoon thyme
Pinch of red pepper flake
Cracked black pepper
1 large onion, chopped
2 slices smoked bacon, chopped
4 cloves garlic, minced
1 teaspoon salt
1 large bunch turnip greens, chopped (cooked down, this will be about 3 cups)
4 cups chicken broth
1 tablespoon balsamic vinegar
Pinch of sugar
6 cups blanched black-eyed peas
16-ounce can diced tomatoes
3–4 links sliced kielbasa
Up to 2 cups water

BURNT-ENDS BEEF BRISKET

This one is from Chef Carl T. Akins, who knows his way around some brisket. Brisket, of course, is more common in Kansas City and Texas than in Tennessee, but there is absolutely no denying its growing popularity in this part of the country or that it shows up on menus at Tennessee barbecue joints regularly these days. Chef Carl's version is pretty darned delicious, if I do say so myself.   **Serves 12–16**

Rub

½ cup salt

1 cup brown sugar

1 cup white sugar

⅓ cup chili powder

¼ cup paprika

6 tablespoons black pepper

3 tablespoons onion powder

3 tablespoons garlic powder

3 tablespoons ground cumin

1 tablespoon cayenne

1 (10–12-pound whole, packer trim beef brisket)

1. Sift all of the rub ingredients into a medium bowl and mix well. Set aside.
2. Trim all the hard fat from the brisket. Trim all the soft fat to ¼ inch.
3. Place in deep pan, apply rub, cover with plastic wrap and foil, and place in fridge for 72 hours.
4. Prepare a smoker or a grill, following manufacturer's directions. Stabilize the temperature at 220°F. Use a mild wood, such as hickory or cherry, for the smoke flavor. Add additional rub generously; cover all sides of the brisket with the rub and gently massage it in. Reserve the leftover rub. Smoke the meat for about 1 hour per pound. For example, a 10-pound brisket may need to smoke for about 10 or more hours. Monitor the internal temperature. When the brisket reaches 170°F–185°F on an instant-read thermometer, in the flat part of the brisket, remove the brisket from the smoker.
5. Separate the point of the meat from the flat. At this time, you can slice the flat part of the brisket and eat it. Trim the visible fat from the brisket point and coat it with the reserved rub. Return the meat to the smoker and continue cooking until the internal temperature of the brisket point reaches 200°F. Remove the brisket from the smoker to a cutting board and let it sit for 10–20 minutes. Cut into chunks and transfer them to a serving platter. Serve it hot with your favorite sauce on the side.

BRUNSWICK STEW

I turn to the incredible Miss Daisy King for everything, and this recipe originally appeared in her book *Miss Daisy Celebrates Tennessee*. She graciously gave me permission to use it, as Brunswick stew is very popular in barbecue restaurants, especially here in Middle Tennessee. This one is easy to make at home. (Special thanks to Justin Stokes for all the help.) **Yields 12–16 servings**

Assemble all utensils and ingredients. Cut the chicken into pieces and simmer in the water seasoned with bay leaves, onions, salt, and black and cayenne peppers until the meat can be easily removed from the bones—about 2½ hours. Remove the chicken from the broth; dice and set aside, removing bones. Add the vegetables to the broth, except potatoes. Add remaining seasonings. Cook slowly for about 6 hours. Add back in diced chicken and cook another hour. One-half hour before serving, add potatoes and cook until they are tender. This stew benefits from slow cooking; the flavor improves if it sets overnight and is reheated.

1 (6-pound) baking hen

2 pounds chicken breast

3 quarts water

2 bay leaves

4 small onions

1 tablespoon salt

1 teaspoon black pepper

1 teaspoon cayenne pepper

2 (10-ounce) packages frozen sliced okra

4 cups fresh or 2 16-ounce cans tomatoes, diced

2 (10-ounce) packages frozen lima beans

2 (16-ounce) packages cream-style corn or niblet corn

½ cup shredded cabbage

2 tablespoons sugar

1 tablespoon Worcestershire sauce

1 teaspoon hot sauce, such as Tabasco

3 medium potatoes, peeled and diced

DEAD END'S BEANS & SMOKED SAUSAGE

George Ewart at Dead End in Knoxville shared this with me. I think it's a winner. The recipe size is geared for a big barbecue, but you can scale it down to cook for a smaller party. **Yields 100 servings (Plan it for your family reunion. I'd have to double it for the Stewart clan.)**

16 ounces country ham, diced fine

1 cup oil

3 pounds smoked sausage, cubed

1 onion, diced

1 green pepper, diced

¼ cup minced garlic

2 (28-ounce) cans tomatoes (Rotel recommended)

2 tablespoons Tabasco sauce

2 large cans (6 pounds each—commercial size, or equivalent in smaller cans) Great Northern beans

3 large cans (6 pounds each—commercial size, or equivalent in smaller cans) pinto beans

2 teaspoons salt

1 teaspoon white pepper

3 tablespoons chicken barbecue rub (commercial is fine)

In a large pot, sauté ham with oil until crispy. Add the smoked sausage and brown it. Add diced onion and pepper and sauté until the edges are brown. Add garlic, stir, and cook for 1 minute. Add the tomatoes and Tabasco and cook for about 5 minutes on medium heat. Drain the beans and add them. Add water to cover. Add salt, pepper, and chicken rub and bring to a boil. Reduce heat and simmer for 20-30 minutes. Serve, or cool down, place in plastic bags to refrigerate until needed, then reheat.

THE FATTY

No, you didn't read that wrong—that's really what this popular dish is called. This recipe that follows comes to me from my Memphis-resident friend Ray DuBose, but if you put "smoked sausage fatty" into Google, you'll quickly come up with a million and a half variations. According to the story Ray tells me, the fatty (or sometimes "fattie") is a Memphis thing, although at this stage every barbecue region in the country claims it. In the most basic terms, it's a smoked sausage. In more complex terms, it's something the barbecue competition guys started making for themselves, experimenting with types, mixtures, and fillings.

"It started off at barbecue competitions," Ray says. At most of those competitions, the teams are working all weekend, often getting no sleep, so eating while you're smoking your meats is fairly critical if you want to stay on your feet. "The original Fatty was introduced at competitions when cooks wanted to put something on the smoker for breakfast the next morning. They would take their favorite rub and coat a 1-pound chub of breakfast sausage place on the smoker. In the morning they would take it out, slice it up to eat, or put it on some biscuits with jelly."

He adds, "These freeze well wrapped in aluminum foil and reheat in the oven or back on the grill so I usually do 4–8 of these at a time."

Basic Fatty

According to Ray, the most basic version goes something like this.

Feeds two hungry guys or a family breakfast, especially with biscuits.

Take the chub of breakfast sausage (a survey of blogs and food sites suggests Jimmy Dean is the beginner's favorite brand) and take the wrapper off carefully to maintain the shape. Then just sprinkle it or roll it in your favorite barbecue rub and throw it on the smoker at 225°F (or whatever temperature you're smoking at) until the internal temperature hits between 165°F and 170°F. Pull it off, cool it, and you're good to go. "This usually takes about 3 or 4 hours, but go by temperature, not time, since every smoker is different. Let stand 5 minutes before slicing," says Ray.

1 "chub" of your favorite breakfast sausage
Barbecue rub to taste

It all seems pretty simple, so, of course, alternatives and variations on the theme quickly developed. If you're on Pinterest or any social media, you've probably seen a popular elaborate version on your feed at some point, involving a fatty that had been stuffed with cheese and lattice wrapped in bacon, then prepared on a grill. That one seems to make the rounds every few months, with a wide variety of attribution.

The variations toy with whatever your tastes are, according to Ray. "Also people will flatten out the sausage rolls and stuff them with spinach and cheese, pepperoni and cheese— or just whatever sounds good. I saw a guy who did a chicken cordon bleu version on a barbecue forum. Wrapping in bacon is very popular."

Alternatives to pork breakfast sausage include ground beef, ground chicken, mild or spicy Italian sausage (pork or turkey), ground lamb, or a blend of any of those to meet the taste profile you aim for.

Filling options are also limitless, based on the cook's imagination. A quick survey of barbecue sites offers a mix of cheeses, vegetables, garlic, honey, spicy peppers, mushrooms, garlic cloves, peppers and onions and more. Moist ingredients in the center seem to be typical, aiding to keep the meat from drying out.

The references to other dishes—Ray's chicken cordon bleu, a pizza version filled with tomatoes, mozzarella and pepperoni, a Greek version with goat cheese, garlic, and spinach— all underline the ease with which a barbecue favorite can be melded with a more traditional dish. A few cooks online suggest wrapping small fatties in Pillsbury biscuit or crescent roll dough and cooking your own sausage and cheese sandwiches. The possibilities are wide.

For those who aren't necessarily looking to prepare them for a barbecue competition, they're great to have on hand for family events and the like. "Usually when I'm smoking I'll throw four or five on the smoker. Then we'll have one for breakfast and I'll throw the others in the fridge or freezer, then just pull them out and warm them in the oven. The great part is it renders out most of the fat so you're left with a meat log," says Ray.

They're perfect to take to picnics, family outings, camping and so on—which is where many or Ray's end up. "We take them to events wrapped in aluminum foil as well and just throw them down on the side of a fire in the morning. Then you just slice them up for breakfast with whatever you want."

Bacon BBQ Fatty

When the "Bacon Explosion" started making rounds on Facebook, Twitter, Pinterest and Tumblr a year or two ago, people started experimenting with the Fatty themselves. The first experiment involved adding bacon to it. That variation is below, also courtesy of Ray DuBose.

Ideal size for a large family breakfast, for about 6 people.

1. Remove the chub of sausage from plastic, keeping the shape of chub. Coat the chub in the barbecue rub. Take your bacon and weave it together into a basket weave shape. Wrap the sausage with sheet of woven bacon with the seam side down (you can remove slices of bacon to get a better fit around the sausage if you need to do so).

2. Place on your smoker at 225°F and leave it until the internal temperature is between 165°F and 170°F. (Optional: Every 45–60 minutes, spritz the fatty with apple juice on the outside of the bacon to help it stay moist and keep it from charring too much. Also optional: You can brush a light coating of barbecue sauce over the bacon 45 minutes or so before you are ready to pull it off smoker.) Let the fatty stand 5 minutes before slicing.

1-pound chub of breakfast sausage
Favorite barbecue rub
1 pound bacon
Optional—your favorite barbecue sauce, spritzer bottle with apple juice (apples and pork pair very well as flavor profiles)

Stuffed Fatty

The stuffed fatty was the next step in the evolution of the recipe for most of us from the bacon version. There is no limit to what you can stuff a fatty with, and if you do a quick search on the Internet for "Stuffed BBQ Fatty," you will find hundreds of recipes. This is as easy to make as the ones that preceded it. **Feeds 5–6**

1 pound chub of breakfast sausage

Stuffing of Your Choice

Popular stuffings include:
  All kinds of cheeses
  Peppers, including jalapeños and poblanos
  Spinach
  Asparagus
  Pizza toppings
  (You name it, someone has made it)

Favorite barbecue rub
1 pound bacon
Spritzer bottle with apple juice
Optional—your favorite barbecue sauce

1. Remove the chub of sausage from wrappings and place it into a zipper-style closure plastic bag and roll the sausage out flat. Cut the bag down its sides and remove the flat rectangle/square of sausage (either leave it on top of the plastic bag or move it to a sheet of plastic wrap or waxed paper).

2. Cover the sausage with whatever ingredients you want to stuff it with and then roll the sausage back up into a roll, sealing the ends, and coat with your rub.

3. Weave your bacon into a basket weave and cover your stuffed sausage roll.

4. Place it on the smoker until the internal temperature reaches 165°F–170°F. (Optional: Every 45–60 minutes, spritz the apple juice on the outside of the bacon to help it stay moist and keep from charring too much. Also optional: Brush a light coating of barbecue sauce over bacon approximately 45 minutes or so before you are ready to pull it off the smoker.) Let stand 5 minutes before slicing.

JASON'S RUBS & MARINADES

Another good chef friend of mine, Chef Jason Little, lives in Knoxville, though he comes to Tennessee from the state of Louisiana and brings his Gulf Coast sensibilities with him. Jason is the only person I know besides myself who is willing to crawl through all the briars to get a bucket full of wild blackberries (they're very common along the roadside and in the fields of Tennessee in early summer). Then he'll show up at my friend Vincent Farone's house, where we're all cooking with a dozen jars of home-made blackberry syrup to die for and mix your cocktails with it.

Jason has been a cook for most of his adult life, and he's agreed to share his take on seasonings and prepping your meats.

"First off let me give you my dry rub seasoning blend," he says.

Chef Jason Little's Dry Rub

Yields enough for two butts or a couple of racks of ribs

You can add 1 ounce cumin and 1 ounce chili powder for a little more Southwest-style flavor if you're doing a Texas-style preparation. Chef Jason says, "I give this recipe out and people have tweaked it for their own taste—they'll add in more sugar, less salt—whatever they prefer. It's a good base to start from."

2 cups brown sugar

1–2 ounces salt (start off with 1 ounce and add the extra if you like more)

2 ounces pepper

1 ounce onion powder

1 ounce garlic powder

Jason's Thoughts on Marinades

"Although I would never drink it, I love to use Mountain Dew to marinate ribs in overnight, Jason says. "I like to use root beer, brown sugar, Worcestershire sauce, and Tony Chachere's spice mixture (available at your grocery or at tonychachere.com) to brush the meat when it's on the grill. Don't ask me for proportions on this one, though—it's a 'looks good to me' kind of thing. You use your own judgment when you're cooking."

On Smoking Meats

Asked about his take on smoking meats and barbecue, Chef Jason says, "Well I don't want to repeat what everyone else will tell you, but slow and low. The judging guidelines they use at competitions can be a good guide to just what this means—they have some fairly specific guidelines, and they're there for a reason.

"Our friend Vincent Farone [see the "So You Want to Be a Barbecue Star" chapter] is one of the few nonprofessionals that I know of that has truly perfected his art when it comes to smoking. We plan on doing some curing of bacon and salt pork during 2014 and 2015. I will make some Tasso as well."

On Grilling Sausages

"On sausage, how many times have you seen someone try to cook sausage on the grill only to later see burnt outside and raw inside? Poach the sausage in water or, better yet, cheap beer, then put it on the grill."

On the Difference Between Grilling, Barbecue, or Smoking

"It's all in the timing," says Chef Jason. Time and temperature tell you what you're doing.

Grilling: Start it on high heat, and you hear a loud sizzle when you put the meat on it. Steaks, pork loin, boneless chicken breast, it doesn't matter—in 30 minutes or less, everything is done, and we are eating.

Barbecue: This is low heat; bone-in chicken, pork roast, burgers/dogs, and the occasional sausage if done right (yes, you can do sausage barbecue without poaching—just too many times people want to throw things like raw "brats" on a hot grill). Depending on what's on the barbecue, reaching eating time takes 2–6 hours.

Smoking: Very low heat. Depending on what kind of setup you have, you can anticipate anywhere from 8–24 hours, depending on what you are smoking.

PULLED PORK WITH HOMEMADE RUB

This recipe, and several more in this section, all come from my friend, Chef Carl Akins.

Carl is a Florida native who has come up through the culinary ranks working across the US. He has spent a lot of his time working in restaurants—"I put myself through college that way. I started as busboy, then waiter, prep cook, grill master, line cook, fry cook, sous-chef, and head chef to restaurant manager," he says.

Carl's formal training came at Stetson and Cordon Blue in Orlando, Florida, accompanied by plenty of on-the-job training. I met him through a historic reenactment organization, where he's also mastered Renaissance and earlier European meals and cooked for groups anywhere from 50–1,000 people (as a *hobby*—that should define his dedication right there, the man is amazing).

He's currently specializing in private catering and making an impact with the food truck craze (look for him on the Food Network's *Great Food Truck Race*). His culinary skill is as good as it gets, and his travel all over the country is a reminder of just how good regional cookery makes its way across the nation—and why we're having a resurgence of good southern-style food in places like Brooklyn, Detroit, and Portland as well. Chef Carl resides in Florida after some cross-country travel, and right now his biggest passion is doing volunteer cooking and support for his local VFW. I hear he's even organizing some swing dance classes for them.

Pulled Pork

The key addition to a barbecue meal: Pulled pork is always welcome.

Chef Carl's Rub

(Carl calls this a Kansas City–style rub himself, but it's close to a whole lot of Memphis rubs as well. You need not use a rub, but this one is tasty and will add plenty of good savory flavor. Keep on hand and use this on everything; this amount should serve for quite a few pork butts. Use according to your discretion, light or heavy)

2¼ cups paprika (for color, blend mild and hot)

1 cup brown sugar

2 tablespoons celery salt

1 tablespoon garlic salt

1 tablespoon dry mustard

1 cup black pepper

2 tablespoons onion powder

1 tablespoon powdered vegetable oil

5 cups kosher salt

3–5 pounds pork shoulder, rinsed with cold water

Use 6 cups hickory chips or chunks, soaked for 1 hour in cold water to cover and then completely drained, to smoke on your grill.

1–1½ cups vinegar sauce

1. If using the rub, combine the mild paprika, brown sugar, hot paprika, celery salt, garlic salt, dry mustard, pepper, onion powder, powdered vegetable oil, and salt in a bowl and toss with your fingers to mix. Wearing rubber or plastic gloves if desired, rub the spice mixture onto the pork shoulder on all sides, then cover it with plastic wrap and refrigerate it for at least 3 hours (preferably up to 8).

2. If not using the rub, generously season the pork all over with coarse (kosher or sea) salt and freshly ground black pepper; you can start cooking immediately.

3. Set up the grill for indirect grilling and place a drip pan in the center.

4. If using a gas grill, place all of the wood chips in the smoker box and preheat the grill to high; when smoke appears, reduce the heat to medium.

5. If using a charcoal grill, preheat the grill to medium-low and adjust the vents to obtain a temperature of 300°F.

6. When ready to cook, if using charcoal, toss 1 cup of the wood chips on the coals. Place the pork shoulder, fat side up, on the hot grate over the drip pan. Cover the grill and smoke cook the pork shoulder until fall-off-the-bone tender and the internal temperature on an instant-read meat thermometer reaches 195°F, 4–6 hours (the cooking time will depend on the size of the pork roast and the heat of the grill). If using charcoal, you'll need to add 10–12 fresh coals to each side every hour and toss more wood chips on the fresh coals; add about ½ cup per side every time you replenish the coals. With gas, all you need to do is be sure that you start with a full tank of gas. If the pork begins to brown too much, drape a piece of aluminum foil loosely over it or lower the heat.

7. Transfer the pork roast to a cutting board, loosely tent it with aluminum foil, and let rest for 15 minutes.

8. Wearing heavy-duty rubber gloves if desired, pull off and discard any skin from the meat, then pull the pork into pieces, discarding any bones or fat. Using your fingertips or a fork, pull each piece of pork into shreds 1–2 inches long and ⅛–¼ inch wide. This requires time and patience, but a human touch is needed to achieve the perfect texture. If patience isn't one of your virtues, you can finely chop the pork with a cleaver (many respected North Carolina and East Tennessee barbecue joints serve chopped barbecue). Transfer the shredded pork to a nonreactive roasting pan. Stir in 1–1½ cups of the vinegar sauce, enough to keep the pork moist, then cover the pan with aluminum foil and place it on the grill for up to 30 minutes to keep warm.

9. To serve, mound the pulled pork on the hamburger buns and top with coleslaw. Let each person add more vinegar sauce to taste.

GRILLED CORN ON THE COB WITH BARBECUE BUTTER

This is another of Chef Carl Akins's fantastic recipes and one that's easy to try with or without barbecue as your main course. I have found in experimenting that it goes well with a nice grilled steak just as well as with some brisket or pork butt. The herb butter just adds a richness of flavor that can't be beat, and in the barbecue butter, there's a little heat to it that reminds me of Louisiana and Southwest or Tex-Mex–style cooking.   **Serves 8**

1. Heat the grill to medium.
2. Pull the outer husks down the ear to the base. Strip away the silk from each ear of corn by hand. Fold husks back into place and place the ears of corn in a large bowl of cold water with 1 tablespoon of salt and ½ cup sugar for 10 minutes.
3. Remove the corn from water and shake off excess. Place the corn on the grill, close the cover, and grill for 15-20 minutes, turning every 5 minutes or until kernels are tender when pierced with a paring knife. Remove the husks and eat on the cob or remove the kernels and place in a bowl for serving. Serve with the Barbecue Butter and/or Herb Butter. Spread over the corn while hot.

8 ears corn

Kosher salt

½ cup sugar

Barbecue Butter, recipe follows

Or, Herb Butter, recipe follows

Barbecue Butter

Chef Carl provides this for 8 ears of corn; I found it works for up to 12.

2 tablespoons canola oil

½ small red onion, chopped

2 cloves garlic, chopped

2 teaspoons Spanish paprika

½ teaspoon cayenne powder

1 teaspoon toasted cumin
seeds

1 tablespoon ancho chili
powder

½ cup water

1½ sticks unsalted butter,
slightly softened

1 teaspoon Worcestershire
sauce

Salt and freshly ground black
pepper

1. Heat the oil in a medium sauté pan over high heat until almost smoking. Add the onion and cook until soft, 2–3 minutes. Add the garlic and cook for 30 seconds. Add the paprika, cayenne, cumin, and ancho powder and cook for 1 minute. Add ½ cup of water and cook until the mixture becomes thickened and the water reduces. Let cool slightly.

2. Place the butter in a food processor, add the spice mixture and Worcestershire sauce, and process until smooth. Season with salt and pepper, scrape the mixture into a small bowl, cover, and refrigerate for at least 30 minutes to allow the flavors to meld. Bring to room temperature before serving.

Herb Butter

There's plenty here for well more than 8 ears of corn. I figure about a tablespoon of butter per ear, if you like serious butter, and that works out to 16. If you don't use it all, it saves nicely in the fridge. I like it with fresh basil from my garden, after experimentation.

2 sticks unsalted butter, at
room temperature

¼ cup chopped fresh herbs
(basil, chives, or tarragon)

1 teaspoon kosher salt

Freshly ground black pepper

Combine all ingredients in a food processor and process until smooth.

GRILLED TARRAGON ASPARAGUS

My friend Michaela Burnham has had quite the life—a professional model who put herself through law school and has served for decades as a public defender all over Tennessee. These days, she lives in Knoxville. She's also one of my favorite foodies, and she shared her take on asparagus, which is utterly delicious. This may seem a little on the hoity-toity side for barbecue, but served up next to pulled pork or sliced brisket, it's a perfect side.   **Serves 4–6**

Preheat grill to medium-hot (charcoal) or medium (gas). Mix all ingredients in a shallow pan until asparagus is well coated with the oil and herb mixture. Grill (covered for gas), turning occasionally, until done with a few brown spots, about 6–8 minutes.

1 bunch trimmed medium-width asparagus

½ cup chopped fresh tarragon

2 tablespoons extra-virgin olive oil

¼ teaspoon salt

⅛ teaspoon freshly ground pepper

SIDE DISH RECIPES

LIB'S CHOWCHOW

In this part of the South, chowchow is a condiment that gets constant use. Most of us have older family members who made it, but with the resurgence of canning, it has come back as a popular staple among younger crowds. Every family, across Tennessee, Kentucky, and Alabama, has a recipe for this relish, which typically uses whatever is left over at the end of the growing season and varies according to preference. Some chowchows are spicy, some sweet, some heavy with tomatoes, and some burgeoning with cabbage and onion. It's eaten on pinto or white beans with corn bread traditionally, but modern southern chefs serve it up on burgers, hot dogs, and fried green tomatoes—and of course, with your barbecue.

If you can, here's a terrific recipe to try, courtesy of the lovely Miss Daisy King, a legend on the Nashville culinary scene. This makes about 13 pint jars of chowchow, so you're ready to give them out to friends and family.   **Yield: 13 pint jars**

1 gallon small green tomatoes
14 large onions
6 hot peppers (such as jalapeño)
12 sweet peppers
2 medium cabbages
6 cucumbers
Salt (and pepper) to taste
9 cups apple cider vinegar
7½ cups sugar
½ box pickling spice, tied in bag

Grind tomatoes, onions, hot and sweet peppers, cabbage, and cucumbers in food chopper or processor. Add salt and pepper to taste (about ¼ cup each). Let drain well. Squeeze out as much liquid as possible with hands. Combine vinegar, sugar, and spice and bring to a boil. Add vegetable mixture and simmer for 30 minutes. Place in hot jars and seal.

OLD-FASHIONED COLESLAW

There are so many variations on coleslaw that it all depends on one's tastes. My husband's father, from Louisiana, mixes both mustard and mayo into his. I have to admit a fondness for vinegar slaw. This is a very traditional, smooth, and creamy Tennessee variation from which you can add or subtract ingredients to get the taste you want. I have two or three variations on this recipe from several sources, all cooks with a long Tennessee pedigree. **Yield: 6–8 servings, more if used to top sandwiches**

Finely chop your cabbage and place it in a bowl. In a second bowl, add the rest of the ingredients and mix well. Pour over the cabbage and mix thoroughly, then cover and refrigerate.*

You can add in a touch of yellow mustard if you want to add that flavor element, but experiment carefully with how much you want the flavor to be impacted. A teaspoon is probably plenty.

*Remember, egg-based mayonnaise does not handle hot days well, so keep coleslaw cool until you're ready to use it if you're eating outside.

6 cups finely chopped cabbage (red or green, your preference; I like red)

1 tablespoon sugar

1 teaspoon salt or to taste

½ teaspoon black pepper or to taste

½–¾ cup mayonnaise, depending on your preference for creaminess

SIDE DISH RECIPES

PANKY'S PICKLES

Everyone in the South used to make pickles. Those of us who still do mostly have recipes handed down from grandmothers and other relatives. It's kind of cool that we're getting back to making them for ourselves. This recipe comes from my friend Melissa Corbin of Corbin in the Dell (corbininthedell.com), who, once again, reminds me what it means to do food right.

This should give you a couple of large or perhaps 4–6 small mason jars full.

3 1-quart jars with lids and
   rings
4 cups distilled water
4 cups white vinegar
4 tablespoons sea salt
3 chile de arbol
5–8 cloves sliced garlic
1 small bunch of dill
3 pounds sliced cucumbers,
   unpeeled

Heat jars in a water bath. Bring water, vinegar and salt to a boil. Place 1 chile de arbol in each jar. Layer garlic, dill, and cucumbers. Pack them in pretty tight. Fill jars with liquid up to the bottom rim of jar. Place lid on jar mouth with rings loosely secured. Place in water bath and process for approximately 15 minutes. Place on cooling rack and tighten rings. As the lids pop, you know they are sealed fresh!

PEG LEG PORKER'S SMOKED GREEN BEANS

This one comes by way of Carey Bringle of Nashville's beloved Peg Leg Porker. Carey is one of my personal barbecue heroes, for so many reasons. I can vouch for just how wonderful this particular recipe is—if you haven't smoked veggies before, this is a good place to start.   **Yield: 35 servings**

1 (10-pound) can of green
   beans (Italian cut)—or 10
   (16-ounce) cans
½ onion cut into slivers
¼ pound bacon, diced
⅛ cup pepper or pepper to
   taste

Mix all together in pan. Smoke for 3 hours.

PUCKETT'S GRO. & RESTAURANT PIGGY MAC

I adore Puckett's. My favorite location is the one in downtown Franklin, not very far from my house. Andy Marshall knows the ins and outs of barbecue, and this barbecue mac and cheese variation is bound to have everyone at your table happy and full. You can find Puckett's sauces online if you wish to use them at puckettsgrocery.com.

Obviously, every restaurant has some take on mac and cheese, but this one is particularly marvelous, layered with pulled pork. It's a meal in and of itself. **Yield: 1–2 servings, intended as a main dish**

Complete Dish

Mac and Cheese

(Note: This will make more
  than you need.)
1 pound elbow noodles
3 cups whole milk
4 tablespoons butter
1 pound American cheese,
  shredded
¾ tablespoon salt
½ tablespoon white pepper
¼ tablespoon Cajun spice
¼ tablespoon granulated
  garlic
¼ cup Asiago cheese
¼ cup shredded cheddar
  cheese

6 ounces pulled pork
1 iron skillet or casserole dish
  (I always opt for cast iron)
1 ounce barbecue sauce
  (Puckett's recommended)
8 ounces macaroni and cheese
  (see recipe below)
⅛ cup Gouda cheese,
  shredded
2 tablespoons Panko or Italian
  bread crumbs
Green onion for garnish

Cook elbow noodles and drain. In a sauce pan, bring milk to a simmer. Add the butter to the milk and then slowly add the American cheese, whisking as you add to allow to melt. Once the cheese is melted, add dry spices and whisk. Pour mixture over drained, prepared noodles. Fold in the Asiago cheese and shredded cheddar at this time.

Piggy Mac Assembly

Place the cooked pulled pork into a small iron skillet or casserole dish. Drizzle the barbecue sauce over the pulled pork, then place the prepared mac and cheese on top of the pulled pork barbecue. Sprinkle the shredded Gouda cheese on top of the mac and cheese. Cover with bread crumb mixture and place in a 350°F oven for 5–7 minutes until the top is brown and the macaroni is bubbly. Remove from oven, garnish, and serve.

SOUTH CAROLINA COLESLAW WITH APPLES

This is a traditional slaw recipe in my family—it came to me from my aunt, Jackie Howell. She tells me that typically, this recipe shows up with regularity at every Fendley family reunion (my paternal grandmother's family) in South Carolina. You find fruit-based slaws in Tennessee as well. This one uses dried cranberries and apple, so those with a sweet tooth will truly appreciate it. I find that apples pair well with pork.   **Serves 6–8**

Mix the slaw, Craisins, and apples. Whip the mayonnaise, milk, sugar, and vinegar together and mix with slaw. Quick, easy, and great with barbecue.

1 bag of slaw mix (about 16 ounces)
½ cup Craisins or other dried cranberries
1 apple chopped in small pieces
1 cup mayonnaise
½ cup milk
1½ tablespoons sugar
2 tablespoons vinegar

SWEET & TANGY COLESLAW

This recipe also comes from Daisy King, but it's a more complex and flavorful take on coleslaw for those who want something more than simple. By the way, Miss Daisy has a number of cookbooks out, and if you really want to learn to cook like a Nashville native, you'll go pick them up. They can be found on Amazon and at Daisy's website (missdaisyking.com). She is absolutely a culinary hero here in the Middle Tennessee area. I have learned more about cooking from her over the years than I can say, and so has everyone who has lived here since the 1970s.   **Yield: 12–16 servings**

1 cup favorite mayonnaise

⅓ cup distilled white vinegar

¼ cup vegetable oil

¼ cup ketchup

2 teaspoons prepared mustard

1 teaspoon Worcestershire
  sauce

½ teaspoon hot pepper sauce

½ cup sugar

¼ teaspoon salt

Poppy seeds

1 head cabbage, chopped

Assemble all ingredients and utensils. Put together mayonnaise, vinegar, oil, ketchup, mustard, Worcestershire sauce, hot pepper sauce, sugar, and salt in the container of a blender or food processor. Process until smooth and well blended. Stir in poppy seeds. Refrigerate until time to serve. Pour dressing over cabbage.

SWEET, SWEET BAKED BEANS

As you may have noticed, Tennessee, especially around Memphis, likes its sauces on the sweet side. That can extend to side items as well. This recipe came to me from my Chattanooga resident friend TJ Vestal; she may be the most foodie-not-foodie-by-profession friend I have. Nothing she has ever made has been less than utterly delicious. **Serves 12–16**

Preheat oven to 350°F. Combine all ingredients except the bacon, mixing well. Place in a large casserole dish and place bacon on top of the bean mixture. Bake for 1½–2 hours.

12 large cans pork and beans
1 cup brown sugar
1 cup ketchup
⅓–½ cup sorghum molasses
1 onion, finely chopped
5 or more strips of bacon

WHITE BEANS

White beans are a Middle Tennessee staple and are actually pretty simple, just a matter of cooking low and slow like barbecue. My variation came about in a very unsouthern way—I started making cassoulet and determined I could make just the beans—and make them well. I cook them in a Dutch oven, but you can just as easily use a covered pan on the stove top if you prefer.

White beans, to be properly served, require some corn bread. I kind of like my corn bread to have the jalapeños in it, which means I tend to leave them out of the white beans as I cook.

Yield: 6–12 servings, depending on the quantity of beans you cook. I usually make a pound for a party of 6.

1–2 pounds white beans

Water

2 tablespoons canola or olive oil

1 ham hock

1–2 jalapeño peppers, slip in half lengthwise and seeded (optional)

Sea salt and black pepper to taste

Chicken broth (optional)

Shredded pork (optional)

Pour your beans into a large mixing bowl, cover with about 3 inches of water over the top of the beans, and soak overnight, at least 6–8 hours.

The next day:

1. In a frying pan, heat your oil and sauté the ham hock until the exterior skin is browned and slightly crispy.

2. Drain the beans thoroughly and place in a deep pan on the stove top, cover with water, and bring to a boil. Lower the heat and allow them to simmer for about 5 minutes. Then add in your ham hock and jalapeños and season lightly with salt and pepper.

3. You may leave them to then simmer on the stove top, but I prefer to cook them in a Dutch oven and place in the oven at about 300°F for about 2 hours, until they are nicely tender.

4. Check the beans and add more liquid if they seem to be drying (I always add a little chicken broth at this point, no more than a cup). Re-season as needed; a little chopped sage or parsley from your garden is nice, as long as you don't overdo it.

5. Allow the beans to cook down in the braising liquid for about another hour. The broth will thicken nicely. Remove from oven, discard ham hock, and allow them to cool somewhat before serving.

6. Ladle over fresh corn bread. Top it with shredded pork, and it's even more delicious.

7. If you're storing them in the refrigerator to reheat later, leave the ham hock in until you've reheated them to serve; leaving them sit overnight in the fridge only makes the flavors richer.

APPALACHIAN BLACKBERRY CAKE

My friend Jenny Barnhill has lived all over and recently moved to Middle Tennessee, where she has taken on chef and catering positions. She has long been an enthusiast about regional cooking, and the following recipe is the sort of thing you might find anywhere along those mountains—from Georgia to Maine—served up as a dessert at the end of a meal.

"It's my understanding that this recipe has been passed down for many generations, in many families, all along the Appalachian Mountain chain," says Jenny. "From Maine to Georgia, summer means a splendid variety of berries that range in color from pale pink to luxurious black. This particular recipe was brought to me by a great aunt in the Champlain region of the New York Adirondacks who would bake it for me as a child after I spent hours picking and gorging on the wild fruit. I passed it on to my son when we moved to Scottsville, Virginia, just east of the Blue Ridge, and discovered that our property was blessed with nearly a half acre of wild thorny vines that bore the dark, sweet berries I had enjoyed as a girl. This recipe works just fine with store-bought berries, but if you are fortunate enough to happen on a wild berry thicket, I believe it tastes even better with fresh-picked fruit." **1 cake, serves 6–8**

1. Preheat the oven to 350°F and grease your Bundt pan. Cream sugar and butter together, then add eggs. Add in dry mix and buttermilk, alternating. Stir in blackberries.
2. Bake 45 minutes. Let cool. Blend together the icing ingredients with mixer while cake is baking and refrigerate briefly to stiffen. When cake has cooled, slather on icing.

2 cups sugar
1 cup butter
4 eggs

Dry Mix

3 cups flour
1 teaspoon each—clove, nutmeg, cinnamon, baking soda, and baking powder

1 cup buttermilk
2 cups blackberries

Icing

1 cup softened butter
1 pound sifted powdered sugar
1 teaspoon pure vanilla extract
3 tablespoons cold black coffee

CHEF JASON'S CUSTARD BANANA PUDDING

The simplest banana pudding recipes I have always involve making vanilla pudding (Jell-O brand is fine, but never instant! Except I know plenty of folks these days who use instant.) as your base, but this very special one uses an old-fashioned egg custard. I suspect that has a good deal to do with Jason's New Orleans background. While it's a bit more complex to create than the standard version, it will absolutely wow your guests—or just your family. I highly recommend making sure you use a real vanilla extract and not an imitation, by the way. You'll be much happier. I tried it with a handmade bourbon vanilla made by my friend Abby Stranathan in Kentucky, and the results were outstanding.

Makes a large casserole, serves about 24

The Custard

8 eggs

8 egg yolks

1 cup sugar

1 quart heavy cream

1 tablespoon vanilla extract

Using a double boiler, combine all ingredients and cook on the stove top, stirring continuously until the temperature reaches 170°F. Remove and chill.

The Banana Pudding

1 (12-ounce) can sweetened condensed milk

1 pint heavy cream, whipped to firm peaks—Jason says, "I choose not to sweeten the cream since there is sugar in the condensed milk."

24 ripe bananas

3 (12-ounce) bags vanilla wafers

1. Combine custard and condensed milk and then fold in the whipped cream. Slice bananas and set aside.

2. In a large casserole dish, start layering. ("I like to start with the cookies then custard mix then bananas," says Jason.) Repeat layers.

3. You can take the egg whites and make a meringue if you like.

Easy Banana Pudding

Aside from the fact that Jason's custard version is luscious and gorgeous, there are moments when you don't have time to put all that together. That's okay. One great secret we all have is our grandmothers' quick versions that were standard in the 1950s, 1960s, and 1970s. One thing I always heard from family is that while you could use pudding mixes, you should never, ever use instant. Well, at the risk of scandalizing everyone, you can indeed use instant, if you're on the spot. (Quit looking at me like that Aunt Jackie!)

Here's the easiest variation there is, when you have guests coming and don't know what to do for them. I have this written down in my little personal recipe book, but I think it came from a yellowed magazine clipping that might have been my mom's.

This serves 10–15 people, depending on serving size.   Plan for 10: Everyone eats more than they think they will.

1. Prepare the pudding according to the instructions on the box. Let it stand a few minutes before making your pudding. Then, in a standard casserole dish, first put down a layer of vanilla wafers, then a layer of pudding (about half your total), then a layer of banana slices. Repeat the layering process. Cover the top with your whipped cream or whipped topping. Cover with foil or plastic wrap and refrigerate for at least 3 hours.

2. If you want to do it the really quick-and-dirty way, buy premade vanilla pudding, and you have no mess, no fuss. (This is, of course, a last resort, and you never admit to it publicly.)

2 regular-size packages instant vanilla pudding OR 2 packages vanilla pudding mix (long-cooking variety)

Milk, amount per box directions on pudding

1 box vanilla wafers (buy name brand; do not buy generic, trust me)

3–4 sliced bananas

1 container (8 ounces) premade whipped cream or your favorite whipped topping

MEMPHIS BUTTER COOKIES

My Memphis friend Ray DuBose and his wife Charlotte shared this recipe for Memphis butter cookies with me. They've been sold in the Memphis city school system for decades, and their popularity meant that there are still commercial firms making something similar today. You can find either commercially packaged versions or house-made versions in many of the barbecue places in the area. Ray tells me the original version, published about 20 years ago in the *Commercial Appeal,* was actually made with margarine, but I think sticking with butter sounds like a good idea. A butter cookie ought to have a little butter. **Yield: 6–7 dozen cookies**

7 sticks butter (or margarine)
2½ cups sugar
6½ cups self-rising flour
1¼ teaspoons vanilla

In a large mixing bowl, cream butter with mixer until light and fluffy. Add the sugar, then cream together until light and fluffy. Slowly add flour and vanilla, mixing to blend thoroughly. Drop the cookies by the tablespoon onto ungreased cookie sheets. Bake at 350°F for 7–10 minutes.

PECAN PIE/DERBY PIE

You're in the South, so expect pecan pie. And be very happy about it. I make this a lot in the spring. More often than not, a shot of Jack Daniel's or a good Kentucky bourbon makes it into the pie as well.

Yield: 6–8 servings

1. In a large bowl, cream the butter and sugar. Add the eggs, pecans, salt, vanilla, and corn syrup. Mix well. Pour into unbaked pie shell (the pecans will make their way to the top of the liquid). Bake in a 350°F oven for 50–60 minutes.
2. To turn this into what we call "Derby Pie," one of the popular variations dreamed up for the Kentucky Derby, pour in about 1 cup semisweet chocolate chips (I like Hershey or Nestlé). The chocolate gets melty on the bottom, then stays semi-gooey after the pie has cooled.

¼ cup butter, softened

½ cup sugar

3 eggs, slightly beaten

1½ cups pecans

⅛ teaspoon salt

1 teaspoon vanilla extract

1 cup light corn syrup

1 (9-inch) pastry shell (store bought is acceptable in a pinch; I use Pet-Ritz brand)

(Optional—about 1 cup semisweet chocolate morsels)

FRUIT TEA

Since I've moved to Tennessee, I've been surrounded by variations on fruit teas. This one also comes from my friend TJ, and it's one you'll find amazingly refreshing on a hot day.

2 cups sugar
2 cups water
8 tea bags
1 quart hot water
2 quarts cold water
2 cups orange juice
¾ cup lemon juice

Boil 2 cups of sugar and 2 cups of water together for 5 minutes to make a simple syrup. Steep tea bags in 1 quart of hot water for 10 minutes. Add tea mixture to 2 quarts of cold water; add orange and lemon juice. Serve over ice. Makes 1 gallon of fruit tea and keeps well.

SOUTHERN SWEET TEA

Oh, my friends north of the Mason-Dixon Line, I do understand the value of some good unsweet tea, but down here, sweet tea is drunk universally. You absolutely cannot go through the drive-through line at the barbecue joint or fast-food place and just say "give me a large tea" without making sure you specify if you DO NOT want sweet. We drink sweet tea, we drink it from childhood. My grandparents made sure we had it at the dinner table as little kids.

There are plenty of variations to the making of that tea, some with extra flavor, some made as "sun tea." (If you don' live in the South and didn't live through the 1980s, you might not know what this is, but I'll explain.)

The simplest way I learned is using 3–4 Lipton family-size tea bags in about 2 quarts of boiling water. The tea was then moved to a gallon pitcher with 1–2 cups of white sugar poured over it while still hot and stirred to dissolve the sugar, then the pitcher topped with cool water. The tea bags stayed in to soak until the tea was a deep, dark brown.

Later, my grandmother Stewart would make sun tea, using a gallon glass jug with tea bags and sugar added, thoroughly covered to keep out bugs, and left to heat in the sun on the porch all morning in the Virginia summer heat. Once it had achieved heat and color, it came in and cooled before serving it over ice at dinner.

Taking a survey, most of my friends with similar backgrounds say the same thing. The type of tea bag is up for debate.

"I don't measure the water. I just use 3–4 family-size Luzianne tea bags in a boiler of water," says Dion Grimes of Birmingham, Alabama. "I boil the water, drop in the tea bags, steep for an hour then pour into a gallon container, add 1 heaping cup of sugar, maybe a cup and a half, then top off the gallon with cold water. Then, I refrigerate until cold."

Charlotte Baker of Mobile, Alabama, says, "Almost exactly like Dion's: Luzianne tea bags are a must, and I add a generous pinch of baking soda to the water, just before adding the tea bags, to prevent any bitterness and ensure clarity. Instead of a heaping cup of sugar, I use a scant cup."

My friend TJ Vestal says, "I put one cup of sugar into a glass half-gallon jug (one that I have used specifically for sweet tea making for over 20 years now) and add about a quart and a half of boiling water and stir it with a long wooden utensil (usually a chopstick) to make certain the sugar dissolves completely in the water. Then I add 2 or 3 family-size Luzianne tea bags (depending on where my guests are from) and let it steep until the jar has cooled but is still warm to the touch. I remove the tea bags and top off the jar with tap water and seal. When the lid pops, it goes in the fridge. This is how a lady from way

DRINK RECIPES

south southern Georgia taught me to make it. It is as sweet and dark as Coca-Cola. People tell me it is excellent, but I don't drink sweet tea myself."

"1½ cups sugar and 9 regular Lipton tea bags," says Sammy Roark of Bowling Green, Kentucky. "Bring the tea bags to a boil in about 8 cups of water. Remove from heat, cover, steep for 5 minutes. Pour sugar into gallon pitcher and add steeped tea. Add cool water back into tea bags and squeeze lightly. Remove teabags and add water to pitcher. Fill to gallon mark with cold water, refrigerate."

"We use the imprecise method here too," says Lisa Roberts Cannady of Knoxville, Tennessee. "Sometimes I add green tea bags to the black tea (Lipton, Luzianne, etc., I'm not picky) in about ½ gallon hot water. I steep for 10–15 minutes, squeezing the bags is a no-no, and add the sugar while the liquid is still warm, then dilute with cool water. I usually use 1 cup of sugar to a gallon. My mom uses 2 cups. I will sometimes do sun tea in a mason jar with fresh mint, herbs, fruit, but there is no precision on that one either."

Lisa is a girl after my own heart. I love mint tea and tend to throw fresh stalks of mint into my tea from the garden as it steeps. But then, I lived in Greece as child, and they love mint tea in southern Europe and the Middle East. I've also been known to make a 1:1 simple syrup boiled with mint to add to my unsweet tea and lemonade.

My friend Shawntel Osborne of Decatur, Alabama, says she sometimes makes hers with Constant Comment tea for a little spicy flavor. I know a lot of people who enjoy that variation.

Steve Corn of McMinnville, Tennessee, says, "I make it by the gallon, 6 big tea bags, 2 cups sugar. Or granulated sweetener that measures the same as sugar and about a cup of lemon juice. I like mine super tart."

I like lemon slices, but the move to the Arnold Palmer style, blending half tea and half lemonade (usually made from concentrate), is also a big southern thing right now.

I have to admit, I don't have as much of a sweet tooth as I used to—I'm more inclined to go unsweet with a little lemon, or a touch of mint or citrus simple syrup for my home drinking.

But sweet tea has been a thing here for years, it will always be quintessentially Southern, and if you want the real barbecue cooking experience, you need a cold glass of sweet tea.

Index